10867257

MOTHER ANGELICA
ON SUFFERING
AND BURNOUT

MOTHER ANGELICA
ON SUFFERING
AND BURNOUT

EWTN PUBLISHING, INC.
Irondale, Alabama

Mother Angelica on Suffering and Burnout was originally published as six mini-books: *His Silent Presence* (1973), *Jesus Needs Me* (1974), *Dawn on the Mountain: The Gift of Dryness in Prayer* (1976), *His Pain — Like Mine* (1976), *Spiritual Hangovers* (1976), and *The Healing Power of Suffering* (1977), copyright Our Lady of the Angels Monastery 3222 County Road 548, Hanceville, Alabama 35077, ww.olamshrine.com, and printed with the ecclesiastical approval of Joseph G. Vath, D.D., Bishop of Birmingham, Alabama, USA.

Printed in the United States of America. All rights reserved.

Cover and interior design by Perceptions Design Studio.

Cover art: detail from official portrait by John Howard Sanden.

All quotations from Holy Scripture are taken from Jerusalem Bible, © 1966 by Darton Longman and Todd Ltd. and Doubleday and Company Ltd.

EWTN Publishing, Inc.
5817 Old Leeds Road, Irondale, AL 35210
Distributed by Sophia Institute Press, Box 5284, Manchester, NH 03108.

Library of Congress Cataloging-in-Publication Data

Names: M. Angelica (Mary Angelica), Mother, 1923-2016, author.
Title: Mother Angelica on suffering and burnout.
Other titles: Suffering and burnout
Description: Irondale, Alabama : EWTN Publishing, Inc., 2017. | "Originally published as six mini-books: His Silent Presence (1973), Jesus Needs Me (1974), Dawn on the Mountain: The Gift of Dryness in Prayer (1976), His Pain—Like Mine (1976), Spiritual Hangovers (1976), and The Healing Power of Suffering (1977)"
Identifiers: LCCN 2016046683 | ISBN 9781682780084 (hardcover : alk. paper)
Subjects: LCSH: Suffering—Religious aspects—Christianity. | Spirituality—Christianity. | Spiritual life—Christianity. | Consolation.
Classification: LCC BV4905.3 .M23 2017 | DDC 248.8/6—dc23
LC record available at https://lccn.loc.gov/2016046683

Contents

EDITOR'S NOTE

This volume brings together for the first time *His Silent Presence, Jesus Needs Me, Dawn on the Mountain: The Gift of Dryness in Prayer, His Pain—Like Mine, Spiritual Hangovers,* and *The Healing Power of Suffering,* six "mini-books" written by Mother Angelica and published by Our Lady of the Angels Monastery in the 1970s. Each section of this book corresponds to one of Mother's original mini-books. Taken together, they form a unique and beautiful work of spiritual wisdom and prayerful reverence.

Mother Angelica wrote these words on a pad of paper while in Adoration of the Blessed Sacrament in the chapel of her monastery in Irondale, Alabama. Her order, the Poor Clares of Perpetual Adoration, has been dedicated to the Blessed Sacrament since its founding, and so it is only fitting that Mother's written works were completed in His Presence.

By the mid-1970s, the Nuns of Our Lady of the Angels Monastery were printing as many as twenty-five thousand copies of these mini-books and others per day. This was truly a nascent mass-media operation, one that would lead to the creation of EWTN—the Eternal Word Television Network.

This book is a faithful representation of Mother Angelica's original work, with only the most basic corrections of printing errors, adjustments to formatting, and so on. You can be confident that you are reading an authentic presentation of the wisdom and spirituality of one of the most important figures in the history of Catholicism in America.

Mother Angelica
ON SUFFERING
AND BURNOUT

SUFFERING

THE HEALING POWER OF SUFFERING

The Purpose

From the time of Adam and Eve man has tried to escape suffering in any form. It is a mystery to all except the holy ones of God. The Prophets saw it as a call from God to repent. The Apostles saw it as "a happy privilege" to imitate Jesus. Pagans saw it as foolishness. Men of today see it as an evil and try to avoid it, but it follows them wherever they go.

Suffering is something we love to talk about when it is ours, but dislike hearing about when it belongs to someone else. We can see it work wonders in the lives of others but have no use for it in our own. We can see the wisdom of God chastising our enemies but think of Him as cruel when we are afflicted. We consider it justice when an alcoholic develops cirrhosis

5

of the liver, but injustice when we are victims of a migraine headache resulting from a lack of trust in God.

We would like to ignore suffering, hide it, and pretend it is not there, but reality forces us to face it in spite of ourselves. Some are made holy by embracing it, and others become bitter and resentful by refusing it. It makes some strong and crushes others. Some will never acknowledge its presence in their lives, but somehow everyone realizes that this game of "pretend" destroys and disfigures the soul.

Many seek to find excuses for suffering by blaming society, people, events, history, greed, and original sin, but their suffering is only increased by this spirit of resentment.

When men are sick they seek a doctor, when they are lonely they seek companionship, when they are poor they seek riches, when they are tense they seek relaxation, when they feel the pangs of guilt they drown it by excesses of one kind or another. When they are cold they seek warmth, and when they are hot they seek the coolness of a morning breeze. Man runs from any form of discomfort or pain, and the words of St. Paul find a place in his heart, "About this thing, I have pleaded with the Lord three times for it to leave me." There are not many who are satisfied with the answer Jesus gave him, "My grace is enough for you: My power is at its best in weakness" (2 Cor. 12:8-9).

Paul was suffering from within himself and from the agonies built into his missionary endeavors, none of which would God lift a finger to lessen. When Jesus told him His grace was sufficient, He meant not only that the grace of God would be with him as strength, but that grace in itself was all Paul was to be concerned about.

There was a purpose for all his trials and the purpose was to increase grace—holiness of life—a "participation in the Divine Nature" (2 Pet. 1:4).

This increase of grace was to be uppermost in the mind of Paul, and he was to trust his Master as to the best way to increase that grace. This is why Paul had to admit "when I am weak then I am strong" (2 Cor. 12:10).

The acceptance of the trials God permitted in his life increased grace in his soul, and that grace made him more like Jesus. When he was like Jesus, he bore these same trials with courage and union with the Father's Will. Like the "one thing necessary" Jesus mentioned to Martha (Lk. 10:42), Paul was not to concentrate on what he was suffering but on the grace with which that suffering filled his soul.

Martha was to take her mind off the burden of her work and do it for the love of Jesus. Paul was to keep his eyes on Jesus and forget how difficult the life of a missionary would be. They were both to remember *who* they were working for and not what that work cost them personally. When they loved Jesus enough to give their lives for Him, they would be assured it was reward enough, for God's grace called them, sustained them, guided them, and would ultimately lead them to the light of glory. The suffering entailed on the journey to so sublime a goal was not to discourage or dishearten them. The suffering was not important — only the grace that accompanied it was of any value.

This truth was so imprinted on the mind of Paul that he once said, "I think that what we suffer in this life can never be compared to the glory, as yet unrevealed, which is waiting for us" (Rom. 8:18). To him, Christians "lived by grace" and this "state of grace" gave them the right to boast of the glory that was to come and the "sufferings that brought them patience, perseverance and hope" (Rom. 5:1-5).

The Christian in the time of Paul did not separate the sufferings that were the result of evil men and those ordained by God. He saw God, as Jesus saw the Father, in every daily event. Suffering to him was like a symphony his soul played to God. He was more concerned with the harmony than with the instruments. He knew God's grace would be with him, and he had no fear. The Christian was assured by Paul that "by turning everything to their good God cooperates with all those who love Him" (Rom. 8:28).

The Christian may suffer unjustly, but if he keeps his eyes on Jesus, God will work wonders in his soul. The glory that is to come is so magnificent, and our souls so imperfect and complex, that only the Creator of our souls knows what is needed for us to "carry such a weight of glory" (2 Cor. 4:17).

As children of a loving Father, we must trust His Wisdom in regard to the kind of cross that is necessary for the purification of our particular weakness. Only He knows the degree of glory He desires for us, and what graces and sufferings are needed to arrive at that sublime destiny. Jesus assured us of the Father's continual Providence by telling us that not a hair falls from our head that the Father is not aware of. A small strand of hair, unnoticed by ourselves or flicked from our shoulder in disdain, is seen by the Father.

His love extends to every cross, every joy, every moment of our existence. There is nothing that escapes His Eye, and

He permits nothing to happen to us that does not have some hidden good within it. "Suffering," St. Paul reminds us, "is part of your training. God is treating you as His sons" (Heb. 12:7).

We cannot choose a cross. We cannot decide what suffering is best for the training of our invisible souls. We must grow strong in a way known only to God, for few of us know ourselves or our weaknesses well enough to choose the suffering best suited to change us. We prefer happiness to pain, health to sickness, plenty to poverty, and success to failure. There are few of us who treasure suffering, and if we had to choose our own cross we would choose the least painful. Such is the wisdom of man in contrast to the Wisdom of God.

The Father chose suffering for His Son from His birth to His death, and Jesus reminded us that the servant is not above the master. If He, as God-Man, had to "suffer in order to enter into *His* Glory" (Lk. 24:26), then we too must suffer in order to prepare ourselves for *our* glory.

God is Love, and He wants to share Himself with us here and in eternity, but the cravings of our nature, the lure of riches, and the temptations of the Enemy all combine to distract, dissuade, and discourage us from our goal. The sufferings of this life not only make our temperament more like the Divine Personality of Jesus, but detach us from the things of this world. This Divine preparation opens our souls to the working and pruning of the Father. Our *degree* of glory, and our capacity for love, for all eternity will depend on our grace at the moment of our death. It is of the utmost importance that we cooperate with the Wisdom of God as He directs, guides, corrects, and gently leads us to the Kingdom.

God's way of leading us is as unique as the personality of each individual. The degree of glory He desires for each soul demands different purification. Since that degree is known only to God, we must trust His Providence. We do know from our limited intelligence and the writings of Sacred Scripture that there are *various kinds* of sufferings permitted by God and destined to change and shape our souls to His Image. We shall look at some of these purifications to determine their purpose and fruit. Suffering heals our souls of weaknesses and changes us when we cooperate with His Will in our lives. There is a purpose for suffering for "The purpose of it is that you may be found worthy of the Kingdom of God: it is for the sake of this you are suffering now" (2 Thess. 1:5).

Preventative Suffering

"Think of what Christ suffered in this life, and then arm your-selves with the same resolution that He had: anyone who in this life has bodily suffering has broken with sin, because for the rest of his life on earth he is not ruled by human passions but only by the Will of God" (1 Pet. 4:1-2).

Peter is saying that physical pain united to the sufferings of Jesus is not only virtuous and grace-laden but prevents the Christian from a life of self-indulgence. One does not need much discernment to realize that sickness has often been the only reason a man does not lead a life totally alienated from God.

Many great weaknesses, that have never been overcome by our love for God, are suddenly terminated by sickness. Persons whose pride and health gave them a feeling of independence suddenly realize how very much they need God when weakness or illness racks their bodies and they are forced to take their eyes off themselves and fix them on the God of love and mercy.

Paul himself bore the fruit of Preventive Suffering. Whatever disgusting illness struck him down at Galatia, it prevented him from leaving and he used the opportunity to preach the

Good News. Physical weakness was one of Paul's many complaints to the Lord, but he realized that God directed his life completely and would use even small indispositions for a greater good (Gal. 4:14).

There is no doubt in anyone's mind that there have been times in life when the disappointment over weather, or a flat tire, prevented an accident or some other tragedy.

How many times have we implored God for some favor with great fervor, only to suffer the most crushing disappointment? Months or years later our hearts break out in prayers of thanksgiving when we look back and realize that the acquisition of such a "favor" would have been disastrous!

We read in the Acts of the Apostles that Paul and Timothy desired to spread the faith to Asia, but the Holy Spirit told them they were not to preach the Word there. In their confusion about where to go they reached the frontier of Mysia, intending to cross into Bithynia, and again the Spirit prevented them from going any farther. This was a disappointment, and the indecision that followed caused these faithful followers of Jesus great pain. In blind faith they wandered from one place to another until "one night Paul had a vision," and only then did they know God's Will in their regard. They were to go to Macedonia

(Acts 16:6-10). The Spirit used disappointment, uncertainty, and frustration to show these men the right path. He did this for the good of the Kingdom and their growth in holiness. We can be sure that as He worked in their lives, He works in ours.

There are three startling examples of Preventive Suffering in the lives of Joseph, Moses, and Paul. Joseph had dreams that someday he would be great, but he made the mistake of boasting to his brothers of his superiority. The results of their jealousy and his future position as treasurer of the great Pharaoh is known to all. The danger in reading this fascinating episode is, we forget the purpose of all the humiliation and suffering endured by Joseph. Both his fame and the salvation of the Chosen People depended upon the suffering that Joseph experienced before he reached the position of authority so necessary to feed his people. God used the jealousy of his brothers, the lust of Potiphar's wife, years in prison, and an ominous dream of Pharaoh to accomplish a sign of His Providence and Love.

It is the same in the life of Moses. Though Moses fared well in the house of Pharaoh, it was only after the fear of reprisal, escape, exile, and a tremendous return to Egypt that Moses was prepared for the awesome mission of delivering his people from bondage. As the Lord once saved His People from starvation through the suffering of Joseph, so He delivered them from slavery through the suffering of Moses. His timidity, coupled with the power invested in him, proved beyond a doubt that God was with him. His task was beyond human strength, and many times he pleaded with God to help him lead so great a multitude. The Exodus from Egypt was joyous, but suffering of all kinds accompanied them and at least once prevented them from returning to the place of their slavery.

In the life of Paul, merely three years after his conversion, he boldly preached to the Jews in Damascus that Jesus was the Lord. This roused their anger to such a degree that they plotted to kill him. What followed was a humiliation that Paul never forgot, but it prevented his murder. The Acts tell us that "when it was dark, the disciples took him and let him down from the top of the wall, lowering him in a basket" (Acts 9:23, 25). This suffering was so deeply imprinted in his memory that when he told the Corinthians of this experience almost twenty years later, one can feel the twinge of pain he felt as he wrote his account. This suffering and many that followed prevented Paul from ever boasting of the gifts, graces, and revelations that God bestowed upon him (2 Cor. 11:32-33). Paul would say from his heart, "In view of the extraordinary nature of these revelations, to stop me from getting too proud I was given a thorn in the flesh, an angel of Satan to beat me and stop me from getting too proud" (2 Cor. 12:7).

Paul uses the phrase "was given" because he realized God permitted this suffering to prevent him from the kind of pride that made Lucifer fall like lightning from his position of glory. We do not know whether this suffering was a disease with sudden and severe attacks of sickness or the opposition of his fellow Jews to the Christian faith. Whatever it was it accomplished its mission and kept a talented, holy, and powerful Apostle humble.

From these few examples we can see that God uses suffering to prevent us from making errors in judgment, committing sin, becoming worldly and proud. There are many other reasons for Preventive Suffering in our lives but these few will suffice to show us that suffering of any kind is capable of keeping us closer to God and renewing our souls. Preventive Suffering heals by keeping us away from danger and evil.

Corrective Suffering

"I am the One who reproves and disciplines all those He loves: so repent in real earnest" (Rev. 3:19). The thought of God chastising is repugnant to most Christians. The reason for this is that they judge God by themselves. When we punish, we do so in a fit of anger and seldom in a spirit of love or justice. Our concept, then, of God's chastisement is one of cruelty—the sadistic enjoyment of a Supreme Being lording over weak creatures. How far from the truth is this concept! Throughout the Old Testament, one can almost feel the Heart of God reaching a breaking point as He pleads with His People not to live outside of His Will—not because He desires all men to do as He says, but because the creatures He made live happier lives when they love their Creator. It is for their sakes and not His that He brings them back to Him by chastisement.

When a man invents a machine, he alone knows the best way to operate and maintain it. The man using the machine may decide not to follow instructions and soon finds the machine broken down or inoperative. He can hardly blame the inventor for the results of his refusal to follow directions. The inventor, who loved his invention and desired it to operate at its best, gave the clearest directions for that purpose. What would be his pain to see the work of his hands handled so badly?

If the inventor attached some type of safety device to make the machine stop before it was completely destroyed, we would say he acted wisely and employed a temporary obstacle to achieve a greater good. It is the same with God: He alone knows what is best for the creature He made. He knows what is necessary to prepare that creature for another existence far superior to the one into which he was created. There are positive steps to happiness, called "Commandments," designed to make His creature operate at the peak of his capabilities.

When the soul disobeys these simple rules, made for a higher purpose, untold suffering ensues. We cannot blame this suffering on God. It is the inevitable result of disobedience.

Even so, God, who watches our unreasonable behavior, brings good out of evil. Only when man deliberately and consistently rejects God's pursuing love does he fall from grace. The beautiful human being, created to the image of God, becomes a grotesque caricature of what he was meant to be.

Unlike the inventor who loves his invention for his own sake, God loves man for man's sake. His love for man is Infinite, and out of every mistake man makes, God brings some good. The suffering incurred by disobedience can be used to purify the very weakness that produced it. This is the chastisement that Scripture says God bestows upon those He loves.

In the 12th Chapter of Hebrews, Paul quotes a passage from Proverbs that says, "My son, when the Lord corrects you, do not treat it lightly; but do not get discouraged when He reprimands you. For the Lord trains the ones He loves and punishes all those He acknowledges as His sons" (Heb. 12:5-6). To Paul it was logical that as a natural father corrects his son, God, who is a more loving and faithful Father, would not permit wrongdoing to go by unnoticed.

Paul reasoned that human fathers were thinking only of this life, and their love could not stand silently when a son pursued a course that was not for his good. How much more is God concerned for the eternal life of the sons who were bought with the Precious Blood of His Son, Jesus?

As each one of us tries to change those weaknesses so un-like Jesus, there is a deep suffering within the soul—a frustration and sometimes anxiety. To possess the light to see the Divine Personality of Jesus, and the self-knowledge to see one's self, is a suffering that sears the soul to its innermost core. There is such a gulf between the soul and Jesus that this realization can either change the soul for good or discourage it. There are many moments in the spiritual life when choosing the wrong direction is disastrous. This suffering of comparison between the soul and Jesus and the fear of not corresponding to His grace, can plunge the soul into a darkness comparable to a deep pit.

The soul is so engulfed in the pain, it does not see the purification. It is not aware of any change taking place. It feels only more weakness and the distance between itself and Jesus widening. It does not realize that the blindness comes from the strong light of God's grace shining upon it. This light brings out hidden weaknesses, changes old ones, and destroys past guilt. The soul is so overwhelmed by its own weaknesses that in desperation it reaches out to God as its only good, its only love. Inordinate self-love is slowly changed into an unselfish love — a love like unto God.

Paul had one of these frustrating moments of self-revelation — this process of Corrective Suffering — when he said, "I cannot understand my own behavior. I fail to carry out the things I want to do, and I find myself doing the very things I hate.... I know of nothing good living in me.... What a wretched man I am!" (Rom. 7:15, 18, 24). Paul did not rest in his miseries as most of us do; he immediately reacted to this self-knowledge in a positive manner. He said, "Thanks be to God through Jesus Christ, our Lord" (Rom. 7:25). He realized that God permitted him to take a long, hard look at himself, and the suffering that resulted from such light brought about a change in Paul. Such a change was wrought that one day he could say, "I live now not with my own life but with the life of Christ who lives in me. The life I now live in this body I live in faith: faith in the Son of God who loved me and who sacrificed Himself for my sake" (Gal. 2:20).

The Corrective Suffering in Paul's life helped to change a strong-willed man into an obedient son of God. What he possessed after this suffering was so much greater than the self-indulgence of the past that he told the Galatians, "I cannot bring myself to give up God's gift [faith]. . . . The Spirit Himself and our spirit bear united witness that we are children of God" (Gal. 2:21; Rom. 8:16). Paul was one with Jesus, and the Faith, Hope, and Love that filled his soul with grace, helped him to "run the race and fight the good fight" until his whole life was lived in and for Jesus (2 Tim. 4:7).

One of the best examples of Corrective Suffering is our Conscience. The small child reaching for a cookie that his mother has forbidden him to eat feels a quiet uneasiness pass over his soul like the touch of an invisible hand. He can feel his soul, for a short moment, recoil from disobedience.

A man who listens to this silent admonisher in his life will be happier; if he does not, the pain increases and he loses his peace. When he consistently refuses to acknowledge the presence of his conscience or the suffering it brings, he kills it and never feels this Corrective Suffering again. One day he will totally reject God.

We must not forget the Corrective Sufferings unconsciously imposed upon us by our neighbor. The command of the New Commandment to love our neighbor provides many opportunities for Corrective Suffering. Both our neighbor's faults and his opinion of us can be a source of suffering. His faults bring out the weak points in our own character and force us to practice virtue. This is the pruning Jesus promised us. He told us that "every branch that does bear fruit He prunes to make it bear more fruit" (Jn. 15:2). Our neighbor is often the tool God uses to prune our poor souls of those hidden and unknown faults in our personality and character. There are not many souls brave enough to prune themselves, so God permits the weaknesses of others to purify us. We are given the opportunity to render to our neighbor the kindness, courtesy, benevolence, and compassion that we cannot render to God.

St. Paul assures us that when we change from a life of self-indulgence we can be sure the Spirit is with us. "What the Spirit brings is love, joy, peace, patience, kindness, goodness, trustfulness, gentleness and self-control. You cannot belong to Christ Jesus unless you crucify all selfindulgent passions and desires" (Gal. 5:22-24). Without a good portion of Corrective Suffering in our lives we do not change and enjoy the freedom of the sons of God.

Repentant Suffering

When Jesus said, "Blessed are those who mourn: they shall be comforted" (Matt. 5:4), He was speaking of the sorrow that follows true repentance. Only those who have fallen deeply understand what the word "mourn" means.

The sinner who suddenly realizes God's love for him, and then looks at his rejection of that love, has a feeling of loss similar to the death of a loved one. A deep void is created in the soul and a loneliness akin to the agony of death. The soul feels wrapped in an icy grip of fear. This is not, however, the fear of punishment but the realization of its ingratitude towards so good and loving a God. Sorrow begins to heal the wounds made by sin, and God Himself comforts the soul with the healing balm of His Mercy and Compassion.

If the sin were great, the soul, humbled by self-knowledge, remembers its weakness so as never to offend God again but forever rejoices in His Mercy. This combination of mourning and comfort keeps the soul in a state of dependence and trust in God, who sought and found His lost sheep.

We see this combination of sorrow and joy in David, Peter, and Paul. After David's sins of adultery and murder God reprimanded him through Nathan the Prophet. David then realized the full extent of his sin, and his soul was crushed under so great a burden. He could not escape from himself or the constant reminder of his offense in the person of Bathsheba, his new wife. His soul cried out to God in an attempt to wash himself clean. "Have mercy on me, O God, in Your goodness; in Your great tenderness wipe away my faults, wash me clean of my guilt, purify me of my sin" (Ps. 51:1-2).

David unburdens his guilt and tells God, "I am well aware of my faults; I have my sin constantly in mind, having sinned against none other than You, having done what You regard as wrong" (Ps. 51:3-4). Here we have the deepest pain in the Suffering of Repentance.

When the soul realizes that the sins it has committed not only affect itself and the community but offend a powerful and loving Lord, it feels a sense of loss for having deprived so good a God of the honor and glory of a virtuous life. The difference between this sense of loss and that which exists in hell is that the Suffering of Repentance reaches up to God for Mercy, while those in hell know only remorse. They possess a hatred of God that fills their miserable souls with bitter regrets and a refusal to seek forgiveness.

Unlike Saul, David acknowledged the Justice of God's chastisement: "You are just when you pass sentence on me, blameless when You give judgment" (Ps. 51:4).

David's repentance recalled his sinner condition, and with a heart overflowing with contrition he reminds God, "You know I was born guilty, a sinner from the moment of conception." His self-knowledge is always coupled with hope and a plea for help. "Yet, since You love sincerity of heart teach me the secrets of wisdom" (Ps. 51:5-6). The wisdom David asked for was the knowledge of those hidden faults that surprised him so often and caused him to fall.

David realized that if the suffering of his repentance was to bear fruit it had to be free of that guilt so laden with self-pity and human respect. "Instill some joy and gladness into me," he petitioned God, "let the bones You have crushed rejoice again. Hide Your face from my sins, wipe out all my guilt" (Ps. 51:8-9).

David longed to be free of guilt, not for his own sake but as a preparation for something better. To him there was nothing greater than to begin again, and so he says, "God, create a clean heart in me, put into me a new and constant spirit; do not banish me from Your Presence. Do not deprive me of Your holy spirit. Be my saviour again, renew my joy, keep my spirit steady and willing" (Ps. 51:10-12).

Man seeks to make up for his sins in some positive way: A thief gives away something to the poor; a man with a temper seeks to be gentle. David realized that accomplishing some good work was pleasing to God, but he knew something that it would be well for us to remember. He understood that the very suffering of his repentance was pleasing to God. "Sacrifice gives You no pleasure," he said, "were I to offer a holocaust, you would not have it. My sacrifice is this broken spirit; You will not scorn this crushed and broken heart" (Ps. 51:16-17).

How many of us understand this profound truth: the suffering heart, broken over its infidelities, broken out of love for so great and good a God, is a sacrifice that rises to Heaven and is accepted by God more than many good works.

The Suffering of Repentance washes us clean, changes our heart, determines a new course, and humbles us before the Lord.

We can see this action in Peter. He had just denied Jesus for the third time, and St. Luke tells us that "the Lord turned and looked straight at Peter." This glance pierced Peter's heart like a two-edged sword, for "he went outside and wept bitterly" (Lk. 22:61-62).

Peter's repentance brought about the suffering born of love. Jesus had warned him and asked him to be vigilant and pray, but Peter's confidence in himself was greater than his dependence upon the Lord, and he fell deeply.

The suffering of his repentance drove him *to* Jesus, while in contrast the suffering of Judas' remorse drove him *away* from Jesus. Peter followed his Lord at a distance, no longer trusting in himself. When news of the Resurrection reached him he ran to the tomb to see his Lord.

There is one simple remark in St. Luke's account of the disciples returning from Emmaus that shows us the efficacy of Peter's repentance. It merely says, "The Lord has risen and has appeared to Simon" (Lk. 24:34). How true is the Beatitude that tells us "the mournful shall be comforted" (Matt. 5:4).

We find the same Repentant Suffering in the life of Paul, former Pharisee and Persecutor. Everywhere he went he witnessed to his conversion and told of the marvelous Mercy of God.

"You must have heard," he told the Galatians, "of my career as a practicing Jew, how merciless I was in persecuting the Church of God, how much damage I did to it" (Gal. 1:13). Paul had not only rejoiced over the death of Stephen; he immediately set out to procure the death of other Christians.

"Saul worked for the total destruction of the Church; he went from house to house arresting both men and women and sending them to prison" (Acts 8:3). He actually went into the homes of his Jewish brethren and literally dragged out in chains anyone who professed that Jesus was the Lord (Acts 22:4).

When the people he imprisoned were being tried and sentenced Paul voted for their death (Acts 26:10). His trip to Damascus was not his first in pursuit of the followers of Jesus. In speaking to King Agrippa, Paul said, "I often went round the synagogues inflicting penalties, trying in this way to force them to renounce their faith; my fury against them was so extreme that I even pursued them into foreign countries" (Acts 26:11).

We can imagine what Paul felt when on one of these trips to inflict punishment he saw a great light from Heaven and heard Jesus say, "Saul, Saul, why are you persecuting Me? It is hard for you, kicking like this against the goad" (Acts 26:14). Saul was being used by the Enemy, and what he thought was zeal was a spirit of darkness.

What a terrible suffering to suddenly realize that everything he fought for, worked for, and taught others to embrace, was wrong and displeasing to God! Wiping out Christians was inflicting insults on God Himself, and all along Saul felt so positive that he was working for the glory of God when in reality he was fighting against Him.

The soul of Saul was surely pierced as if a sword had entered its very core. This pain he never forgot, for he constantly reminds the Christians of his former role as persecutor and the Mercy of God in his regard. This Repentant Suffering kept him ever humble and grateful. "I am the least of the Apostles," he said, "in fact I persecuted the Church of God; I hardly deserve the name Apostle; but by God's Grace that is what I am and the grace He gave me has not been fruitless" (1 Cor. 15:9, 10).

Paul never ceased to wonder at the Mercy of God. "I thank Christ Jesus," he told Timothy, "who has given me strength and who judged me faithful enough to call me into His service even though I used to be a blasphemer and did all I could to injure and discredit the Faith" (1 Tim. 1:12, 13).

Like King David and Peter, Paul's Repentant Suffering, born of love, bore the fruit of joy and gratitude. This Repentance was a source of continual thanksgiving to God, whose Love and Mercy sought out this son in his misguided zeal.

Later in his life, Paul was to see Repentant Suffering bear fruit in the lives of others when he himself was the initiator of that repentance.

The Corinthians had begun to stray from the truth, and Paul reprimanded them severely. He realized his letter of reproach had distressed them but rejoiced because their "suffering led them to repentance." "To suffer in God's way" he told them, "means changing for the better and leaves no regrets, but to suffer as the world knows suffering brings death" (2 Cor. 7:9, 10).

Suffering in itself is neither good nor bad. It is the *way* one suffers and the *fruit* of that suffering that matter. Those of the world suffer only remorse and regret, because their hearts are set on earthly things.

Those whose suffering is the fruit of loving repentance forget themselves and possess the light to see the transitory nature of all created things.

They look up to God for that stability and assurance that comes from the knowledge of God as a merciful Father. Paul, realizing the depths of this purifying suffering said, "Just look at what suffering in God's way has brought you: what keenness, what explanations, what indignation, what alarm" (2 Cor. 7:11).

The suffering that began by misunderstanding, stubbornness, and ambition ended in Repentant Suffering that gave the Corinthians a greater appreciation of their Faith, more vigilance over their weaknesses, better understanding of God's revelations, greater zeal for the Kingdom, and more awareness of how easily they could fall if they lost sight of Jesus. Yes, Repentant Suffering bore great fruit and enabled them to increase in love and humility.

It was so with them, and it is so with us. Repentant Suffering cleanses our souls, brings down upon us the compassion of God, enables us to begin anew, and makes us prayerfully vigilant.

Redemptive Suffering

"This may be a wicked age but your lives should redeem it" (Eph. 5:16).

The word "redeem" means to rescue, set free, ransom, and to pay the penalty incurred by another. We often lose sight of the definition to "set free," and we miss the power of our example as Christians to do exactly that — set our neighbor free.

We must look at this aspect of Redemptive Suffering if we are to understand its role in our daily lives. St. Paul told the Corinthians that, "indeed, as the sufferings of Christ overflow to us, so, through Christ, does our consolation overflow. When we are made to suffer, it is for our consolation and salvation" (2 Cor. 1:5, 6).

Paul did not want the sufferings encountered by being a Christian to discourage or dishearten anyone. He realized that when Christians saw the blessings and grace that poured upon him after his many trials, they would gain courage to suffer in *their* turn. The example of fortitude and fidelity exhibited by this man of God released them from the fetters of fear and cowardice.

Paul knew that Christ's example of every virtue was as redemptive as His death. By the example of his holy life, the Christian was to release and set his neighbor free from the bondage of sin in which he was immersed. Holiness reaches out to touch everyone and gives them the courage to follow in the footsteps of Jesus. The Christian's suffering was acceptable to the Father for the salvation of mankind because he was so united to Jesus through the grace of the Holy Spirit and because whatever he suffered, Jesus suffered in him. "It makes me happy," Paul told the Colossians, "to suffer for you, as I am suffering now, and in my own body to do what I can to make up all that has still to be undergone by Christ for the sake of His Body, the Church" (Col. 1:24). It is Jesus who continues to suffer in the Christian for the good of all mankind.

Whatever we do to our neighbor, we do to Jesus, and all the sufferings our neighbor encounters in his daily life helps to build up the Mystical Body of Christ. To Paul, everything he suffered was for the Christians to whom he preached and for those who were to come. "I want you to know," he said, "that I do have to struggle hard for you ... and for so many others who have never seen me face to face" (Col. 2:1).

What was the purpose of all this suffering for others? "It is all to bind you together in love," he told them, "and to stir your minds, so that your understanding may come to full development" (Col. 2:2).

Paul offered his sufferings for the good of his brethren, the Jews, for he told Timothy, "I have my own hardships to bear, even to being chained like a criminal — but they cannot chain up God's news. So I *bear it all for the sake of those who are chosen*, so that in the end they may have the salvation that is in Christ Jesus and the eternal glory that comes with it" (2 Tim. 2:9-10, emphasis added).

Here we have Redemptive Suffering offered to God for the sake of others. Paul's desire to suffer for his brethren reached almost to extremes, for one day he said, "My sorrow is so great, my mental anguish so endless, I would willingly be condemned and be cut off from Christ if it could help my brothers of Israel, my own flesh and blood" (Rom. 9:2-4). Paul knew that God would never exact that price for the salvation of others but he went to extremes in his desire to suffer for others so they too might come to know Jesus and enjoy His Kingdom.

Paul even thought that God would use his conversion for the sake of others. In writing to Timothy, he said, "Christ Jesus came into the world to save sinners. I myself am the greatest of them; and if mercy has been shown to me, it is because Jesus Christ meant to make me the greatest evidence of His inexhaustible patience for all the other people who would later have to trust to Him to come to eternal life" (1 Tim. 1:15-16).

God would use the manifestation of His Mercy towards Paul as an opportunity for the conversion of other souls. Great sinners throughout the ages would look to Paul for courage and strength. Yes, the suffering and humiliation Paul endured was Redemptive for it freed sinners of fear and made them look to God for mercy.

Jesus told His Apostles at the Last Supper that "a man can have no greater love than to lay down his life for his friends" (Jn. 15:13). Jesus laid down His life for our sake, and He desires that we do the same for our neighbor if and when that opportunity presents itself. A soldier gives his life for his country, and he is a hero because his act of sacrifice is unselfish—he dies that others may live in peace. Most Christians are not asked to make the supreme sacrifice, but God chooses some to participate in the salvation of souls, not by giving up their lives but by enduring sufferings that are over and above what they need for themselves. All those whose suffering is Redemptive can say with St. Paul, "Never lose confidence because of the trials that I go through on your account; they are your glory" (Eph. 3:13).

Every pain we endure with love, every cross borne with resignation, benefits every man, woman, and child in the Mystical Body of Christ. Those who are chosen to bear a greater portion of suffering than others are called by God to heal the souls of many whose lives are bereft of the knowledge and love of God. Redemptive Suffering not only helps poor sinners directly by suffering for them but edifies and consoles good and holy souls as they journey through life striving for holiness. This dual role of Redemptive Suffering merits for those chosen by God for such a role, a glory and happiness in the Kingdom beyond our concepts or imagination. Like Jesus, their sufferings, united to His, rise to Heaven and obtain grace and repentance for those who are straying from God and His Love.

Witness Suffering

The second role of Redemptive Suffering is the powerful Witness it bears to the Wisdom and Grace of God. St. Paul told the Corinthians that the Christian proves he is a servant of God not by charisms but by suffering and virtue. "We prove we are servants of God," he told them, "by great fortitude in times of suffering; in times of hardship and distress; when we are flogged or sent to prison or mobbed, labouring, sleepless, starving. We prove we are God's servants by our purity, knowledge, patience and kindness, by a spirit of holiness" (2 Cor. 6:4-7). He continued to explain that the Christian must be ready and willing to endure anything in his life, be it joy or sorrow.

To see a Christian believe in God's Love when sorrow befalls him gives us Hope.

To see joy on the face of a Christian beset with trials and problems gives us a new concept of Faith.

To see someone crushed but serene over the death of a loved one makes us realize there is another life.

To see sickness and pain carefully borne gives us courage.

To see a friend who has suffered the loss of all material things begin again with trust and love gives us strength to continue on.

To see forgiveness and mercy after friends quarrel brings joy to our hearts.

To see sinners turn to God and rise to great heights of sanctity increases our trust in His Love and Mercy.

No matter what kind or what degree of pain and sorrow we must endure, we are capable of witnessing to the love of Jesus.

The very fruit the Spirit bears in us calls for Suffering. St. Paul says the fruit of the Spirit is love, but it is not always easy to love. Our love must extend itself to the unlovable. We are to be joyful, but we must be detached and possess a great trust in God to maintain joy.

We are to be peaceful, but how difficult it is to maintain a peaceful heart. The Spirit brings patience, but in order to be patient we must choose to be so even when our feelings are anything but patient. We are asked to be kind, good, and trustful. How difficult and painful it is for our poor human nature to be all these good things when our inner being is unkind and suspicious.

Who has not experienced the cost of gentleness? One does not become gentle by some sudden influx of grace. We work at it for days and months and years, and although all is accomplished by the grace of God, our cooperation is necessary.

The last fruit of the Spirit is self-control. This means that my body is under the influence of my soul and the Faith that resides in it. To arrive at that sublime degree of tranquility we must suffer the successes and failures of our weak Will as it strives to give itself entirely to God. Self-control is a gift, but to accept and use it means death to self, and that is the process of Witness Suffering. Our neighbor, who feels within himself all the weaknesses we feel, knows for certain that only God's Grace could make us bear the beautiful fruits of virtue in our lives.

Our example makes our neighbor desire virtue in his life, and the fruits borne of suffering bear witness of the Power and Love of God.

To St. Paul the Witness Suffering of the first Christians was to be so complete that nothing could come between them and God. He told the Romans that "nothing can come between us and the love of Christ, even if we are troubled or worried, persecuted, lacking food or clothing, threatened or attacked" (Rom. 8:35-37).

The Christian is to witness by every kind of suffering in his life, to detachment, the invisible world, the Power of God, the existence of Heaven, the transcendence of God, and the transitory nature of everything in this world.

Paul reminded the Romans that they were to find hope from the examples Scripture gave of how people who did not give up under trial were helped by God (Rom. 15:4-5). The fidelity of the Roman Christian was "famous everywhere," and this Witness of faithfulness in the midst of great trials gave new and old Christians hope and courage.

Even though it is the Spirit of Jesus who bears fruit in us, the struggle within our souls to manifest Jesus rather than ourselves is a great suffering. It is not the unfeeling, unemotional person who witnesses to the Spirit of virtue but the one who chooses to be like Jesus while his inner being wants to indulge in the passion of the moment. The person who is courageous is not the one who feels brave but the one who is frightened and performs a brave action. It is the suffering of a difficult action that bears witness to the Presence of Jesus in our souls.

Witness Suffering is necessary in our lives in order to follow in the footsteps of Jesus. "Take me for your model," Paul told the Corinthians, "as I take Christ." This model was in every facet of his life. "You know how you are supposed to imitate us: now we were not idle ... nor did we ever have our meals at anyone's table without paying for them; no, we worked night and day, slaving and straining, so as not to be a burden ... to make ourselves an example for you to follow" (2 Thess. 3:7-9).

Paul wanted them to realize that he worked hard — "slaved and strained" and suffered from exhausting labor in order to bear witness to how a Christian should act and work.

We will not always be aware we are a witness to our neighbor, but we cannot hide the love of Jesus, and when we love

Him enough to suffer with joy, our lives are like "cities seated on top of a mountain" (see Matt. 5:14)—cities that radiate the love of Jesus to all those groping in the darkness of uncertainty and lukewarmness.

Jesus wants our Witness Suffering to be so strong that we manifest the joy of the children of God by never worrying about tomorrow, being satisfied with our daily bread, seeking first the Kingdom, being poor, meek, and gentle of heart, and dancing for joy when we are abused for His sake. Unlike Redemptive Suffering, which helps our neighbor by carrying his burden *and* ours, Witness Suffering edifies our neighbor and encourages him to take up his own cross and follow Jesus.

Interior Suffering

One of human nature's greatest sufferings is the kind that is within the soul. We call it Interior Suffering. It is difficult because although we can express it to a friend we can never express it on the level of experience.

Everyone has at some time in his life had a headache, and when we complain of one to our neighbor he understands. He immediately relates to that suffering from the storehouse of his own experience. This is not always the case with Interior Suffering, for unlike physical pain dependent upon an organic malfunction, spiritual sufferings are deeply imbedded in an invisible reality—keenly felt and impossible to fully explain.

Physical pain can be measured by degrees and machines, but Interior Suffering is experienced only by the soul and is known only to God.

Its variety is unlimited because each soul's mental, spiritual, temperamental, and intellectual level differ from everyone else's. Each soul is a unique creation from the hand of God, and its sufferings are totally its own.

Physical pain affects the soul inasmuch as the soul reacts either patiently or impatiently with the condition of the body, but interior suffering is spiritual pain.

Resentments, doubts, and lukewarmness eat at our soul and create an emptiness that places us in a spiritual vacuum.

Temperament faults play havoc with our faculties and send our human spirit on a merry-go-round of conclusion and discouragement.

Time lays heavy upon us, and monotony covers us like a fog in the night. Success often brings the fear of failure, and the constant grind of eating, sleeping, and working creates a lethargy that leads to boredom.

Misunderstandings can gnaw at our souls as we seek for solutions to impossible situations.

The remembrance of past sorrows and the prospect of more to come paralyze our souls and place us in a state of near despair.

Perhaps the greatest interior suffering is the kind that strikes us when we thirst for God and then find ourselves deprived of the awareness of His Presence. We can withstand the distress that comes from our imperfections and the coldness of our neighbor, but when God seems so far away there is no greater pain.

We see this interior suffering in Peter and Paul as doubts assailed them regarding circumcision, sorrow over the persecution and death of their converts, the misunderstandings between Christians, and the harassment of fellow Jews. At times they were weary, and Paul speaks of his anguish and weariness of soul as a sting of the flesh.

Interior suffering can be more purifying than any other form of pain because we are forced to cope with it. We can distract ourselves and forget a sprained ankle, but when dryness, weariness, sadness, worry, and fear assail us, they hound us wherever we go.

We must understand why God permits this interior suffering, for at first glance it would seem life provides enough pain to sanctify us.

Daily trials and even physical pain are somehow outside of us, but interior pain, be it spiritual or mental, is deep within and forces us to be patient and practice virtue. Interior trials sanctify us slowly because they have the power to change us for the better. It is in the soul, in our personality and temperament, that change must occur if we are to reflect the image of Jesus.

We may have cancer and be healed, but never change. We may triumph over some disagreeable situation, but never change, but when our pain is inside our soul and we cooperate with God's Grace in using it, then it has the power to change us.

It is in our souls that God does His most magnificent work. The world may look upon the aged, the sick, and the retarded with sympathy, but God's work in their souls, through the power of interior suffering, is doing a greater work than when He created the universe. Only in eternity shall we see the beauty of the soul, and only then shall we realize what great things were accomplished by interior suffering.

We can be sure that:

- ❧ Dryness makes us patient as we seek to love God for Himself.
- ❧ Mental anguish makes us depend upon His Wisdom.
- ❧ Doubts increase our Faith when we act according to our beliefs rather than our reasoning.
- ❧ Fear makes us trust God's Providence and Hope in His Goodness.
- ❧ Anxiety leads us to distrust ourselves and release our problems to an all-loving God.
- ❧ Worry makes us realize our helplessness and instills a desire to throw ourselves into the Arms of His Infinite Wisdom.
- ❧ Discouragement over our imperfections makes us strive for holiness with greater determination.
- ❧ Uncertainty as to our future makes us look forward to the Kingdom.
- ❧ And disappointments detach us from the things that pass and make us look to those that are everlasting.

The suffering from within destroys our pride more quickly than the loss of all material things. The soul begins to feel its weaknesses and tendencies towards evil and places beside this mirror the light of God. It sees clearly who it really is, and pride no longer holds sway over such a soul.

Pride rebels against interior suffering because its roots are being shaken of lies and deception. If we bear that suffering with love and cheerfully acknowledge our weaknesses, the love of God will bring about miracles of grace in our souls. We may look up to God in fear and frustration, but in that helplessness we shall find the Hand of God reaching down to raise us up even to Himself.

Personal Suffering

Suffering is a part of the life of every human being, and there are sufferings peculiar to every age group. We speak of colic in babies, growing pains in adolescents, after-forty spread in the middle-aged, and the fears of Senior Citizens.

There are also particular sufferings peculiar to our temperaments. We speak of a highly nervous person as being sensitive, a calm person as indifferent, an angry person as temperamental, a slow person as lazy, and a quick-moving person as hyperactive. We label actions, people, dispositions, personalities, and temperaments and then go our way with an imaginary solution to their problems. We fail to realize that the person so labeled reacts to situations and people differently than anyone else.

In fact, the same problems or circumstances often bring about opposite sufferings in a group of people. We find this in Scripture regarding the controversy over Circumcision (see Acts 15). St. James and his followers fought to have every convert become a good Jew before he became a Christian. St. Paul fought against such a principle, for the light that he had told him that faith in Jesus saved us, and not adherence to a law.

As James suffered from zeal for the old and Paul from his enthusiasm for the new, poor Peter was completely confused.

James and Paul were strong men who fought for the glory of God, but Peter's temperament had the tendency to vacillate from one position to another. Though there was only one problem for the early Church to solve, these three men reacted to it in different ways, and each suffered keenly from his own position.

Personal Sufferings cause us the most overall pain. Other sufferings come and go, but our temperament and personality stay with us, and the constant change for good or bad in which we find ourselves increases that suffering in our daily lives.

It is this Personal Suffering that people tend to run away from or flatly deny exists. We find some running away from this type of suffering by turning to alcohol and others refusing to face the reality of its existence by ignoring their faults. This is why we refuse to admit guilt when our neighbor accuses us of some temperament defect.

We will never admit simply and frankly that we did lose our temper or patience. We explain our actions as justifiable anger and never admit that someone or something had an adverse reaction upon our personality.

We cannot face the fact that our temperament is defective in any way or is in need of change. Our whole life can be spent dodging ourselves and the lesson that Personal Suffering is trying to teach us.

The way we react to various situations is like a thermometer that measures a fever. Our reaction not only tells us what faults we possess but their degree of intensity.

A medical thermometer tells us that our temperature is either normal or abnormal. It is the same with Personal Sufferings. They tell us whether our reaction was normal when a neighbor insulted us or whether it was abnormal. It is normal to *feel* hurt; it is Christian to go a step further and forgive. It is abnormal, however, if that insult results in bitter resentment geared towards nourishing an uncontrollable hatred.

Like the thermometer that registers 103°F., our reaction registers a spiritual danger point and death if a remedy is not applied quickly.

This is the purpose of Personal Suffering in our lives. It tells us what is wrong with us, and Jesus tells us in His Words what remedy to apply.

If we saw the Hand of God in our moment-to-moment existence we would soon realize that our neighbor is being used by God to bring us out of darkness into a marvelous light. For the most part, our neighbor is not aware that he is a cross to us, but the cross he places on our shoulders is of more benefit to our souls than the compliments of our friends.

A difficult personality, knowingly or unknowingly, has the power to bring out of us hidden weaknesses that would never be brought to the surface otherwise. We rebel against that person because of his effect on us. We resent the surfacing of hidden faults. The person we consider our enemy may well be a friend in disguise, for God will use the weaknesses of others to make us strong. The person who touches off our anger tells us we have a temper—and self-control is in order. The person who tries our patience is telling us that our refusal to wait is in reality a refusal to suffer. The excuses we use for not loving our neighbor are merely a smoke screen behind which we hide a lukewarm love.

The Christian who is unafraid to admit his Personal Sufferings will hear the Voice of God speaking to his soul. The pruning may be bitter, but the dead branches will be cut away as the Vinedresser lightens the weight of the cross we carry.

What is a joy to one person may be a sorrow for another, but both can benefit by seeing the Wisdom of God planning and changing the pattern of their lives to fit the image of His Divine Son.

We all react and respond to weather, tastes, situations, events, and people in different and opposing ways, but God picks up the scraps from the table of our lives so they are not wasted. He uses every small hurt to sanctify and every sorrow to make us new. If we cooperate with His Plan in our lives and accept the duty or sorrow of the present moment with love, then whether that suffering is just or unjust, it will serve as a tool in the Hand of God to change us.

God alone knows us perfectly. We are a mystery to others and to ourselves. We almost stand aside and watch ourselves say and do things our inner self rebels against. Like Saint Paul, we can all say "Every single time I want to do good it is something evil that comes to hand" (Rom. 7:21).

These occasions of disappointment in ourselves bring to light our defects and crush the pride that destroys our souls. Most of these Personal Sufferings, however, never show outwardly, and this hiddenness increases the intensity of the pain. They are lifelong struggles and battles — won and lost — seen only by God.

This is why we cannot judge our neighbor. We may discern his exterior actions as good or bad, but it is impossible to judge his motives, light, effort, or grace. Deep within each of us is a soul ever struggling to be better though it fails often. This hidden cross permitted by God is sanctifying, but we must cooperate with His grace and His work in our lives.

We do not understand ourselves because we are so engaged in the battle. We forget past victories because peace is not in sight. Holiness seems impossible to attain because our pride is ever crushed by our inability to do anything on our own.

Our Personal Suffering, ever with us, constantly reshaping our souls, blurring the perfect vision we have of ourselves, and consistently a thorn in our side, is used by God to give us a new birth, a new creation, an empty vessel that He can fill with the fruits of His Spirit.

Wasted Suffering

"If I give away all that I possess, piece by piece, and if I even let them take my body to burn it, but am without love, it will do me no good whatever" (1 Cor. 13:3).

It is a frightening thought to realize that it is possible to give away everything we possess, suffer the loss and inconvenience of poverty, and all this suffering is of no value.

It is terrifying to hear St. Paul say that the agony and indescribable pain of having one's body burned like a charred piece of wood, is worth nothing also unless it is suffered for and with the love of God in our hearts.

We read further in the Gospel of St. Matthew that Jesus said, "Be careful not to parade your good deeds before men to attract their notice: by doing this you will lose all reward from your Father in Heaven" (Matt. 6:1).

The good works mentioned by Jesus consisted of fasting, prayer, and almsgiving. In each of these good works there is an element of sacrifice and suffering. In each there is pain and detachment, and yet it is possible to do all these good works without pleasing God.

We are reminded of the time Jesus remarked that not all those who say, "Lord, Lord" will enter the Kingdom (Matt. 7:21). We have the tendency to believe that merely *saying* and accomplishing good works is a ticket to Heaven. We forget that just as we cannot *do* anything without Him, we cannot *suffer meritoriously* without Him.

Suffering in itself does not make us holy. If it did, then all those in hell would be saved for they endure great suffering and that pain is eternal—never ending.

It is because Jesus suffered, and we unite our pain to His, that suffering changes and transforms us. It is because His Spirit dwells in our souls through Baptism that He suffers when we suffer. What we do to the least we do to Jesus, and as we inflict pain on others without knowing what we are doing, so we suffer badly not realizing what treasures we lose.

We find a striking example in Scripture of Wasted Suffering in the Gospel of St. John. Jesus told the disciples, "They will expel you from the synagogues and indeed the hour is coming when anyone who kills you will think he is doing a holy duty for God. They will do these things because they have never known either the Father or Myself" (Jn. 16:2-3).

We often lose sight of the interior and exterior suffering of those persecutors whose sole mission was to stamp out Christianity. Jesus calls their suffering wicked and useless. He goes so far as to say these men *never* knew the Father or Himself. Their actions were misguided and their motives insincere. Their suffering and zeal were useless.

In Paul we see misguided zeal but sincerity of heart, and God was able to change his zeal and his heart in a moment.

The Christians who were victims of these persecutors also suffered but how different the result! In the Acts we find the Pharisees suffering so severely from their jealousy and misguided zeal that Stephen's speech about Jesus "infuriated them and they ground their teeth at Him" (Acts 7:54). Wasted Suffering was blinding them to the Truth.

Stephen, however, saw the whole unjust process as an opportunity to witness to Jesus. As they ridiculed him he rejoiced and his face shone like an Angel as he looked into Heaven and saw Jesus standing at the right hand of the Father (Acts 6:15; 7:55).

Stephen felt every stone that brought his life closer to its end, but not a moment of that pain was wasted. He rejoiced, forgave his enemies, and merited the crown of martyrdom.

Whenever we suffer without love it is wasted pain. There are times when doing God's Will or accepting His plan in our lives is difficult or repugnant; but if we accomplish His Will with love He does not ask that we like what we are doing. Love is not a feeling. It rises above the feeling level and desires only the glory of God regardless of personal sacrifice.

True love is built on sacrifice. It grows in time of trial. It is purified by detachment and intensified by suffering.

When suffering does not bear this transforming change in our lives then the fruit is resentment and bitterness. This bitter fruit is a complete waste because it pulls us away from God instead of drawing us to Him.

A heart in need, a broken heart cringing from its wounds, can still offer its pain to God with love as long as it humbly admits God's Wisdom is above its own. Our degree of love is greater when we do His Will though our whole being rebels. Jesus asked the Father three times to remove the Chalice. His fear of what was to come was so intense, He sweat Blood, but not for a moment did His love for the Father's Will weaken.

St. Paul told the Romans, "Nothing can come between us and the love of Christ, even if we are troubled or worried or being persecuted, or lack food or clothes or are threatened or even attacked" (Rom. 8:35).

How many of us can say that? When we are troubled we lose hope; when we worry we become discouraged; when we are persecuted we run away; when we are deprived we rebel. Two people can suffer from the same trial and obtain opposite results. We see this in the suffering of the two thieves crucified with Jesus. Both were guilty of great crimes, both sentenced to the same punishment, both hung on a cross, tortured in every part of their body, and yet the suffering of one was a waste and the suffering of the other purifying. The one cursed the day he was born and the other patiently waited with humble resignation for the moment he would enter the Kingdom of his suffering Redeemer.

It often happens that the wasted suffering of a bad life makes a soul realize the shallowness of its life and leads that soul to repentance. But if our lives are spent in an effort to do our own will on every occasion, if trials and pain are received with bitterness and pride, then the suffering we experience is wasted and our torture is in vain.

If we could only say in our hearts, "Jesus, I accept the sufferings in my life with the same love with which You accepted the pain in your life. I do not understand Your plan, but I trust Your Love and my love reaches to You in the hope of being lost in Your embrace!" We must ask God for the grace to trust His guiding hand and to give us the strength to desire our cup of sorrow with the same love and thirst He desired to die for us.

Jesus and Suffering

"I have come to bring fire to the earth, and how I wish it were blazing already! There is a baptism I must still receive, and how great is My distress till it is over" (Lk. 12:49-50).

The fire Jesus referred to was not the Holy Spirit, whose grace would change and transform our souls. The fire He desired to kindle was the love that came from His Heart on the Cross.

Jesus was truly distressed as He saw so many look upon the Cross as a curse. He took what was considered the personification of the wrath of God and made it a means of Redemption, a solace in times of trial, an anchor in time of sorrow.

In the time of Moses all those who were bitten by the serpents as a punishment from God were healed by gazing at a brazen serpent suspended from a standard (Num. 21:9). The very thing God chose to chastise His people He also used to heal them.

This prefigured what was to come, for Jesus took suffering, the very thing that was held as a curse from God, a sign of His chastisement — and desired it, caressed it, and offered it back to us as a means of healing.

Jesus knew that once He, the Son of the Father, was stretched out upon the Cross, all men of faith would obtain the strength to endure the sufferings the Father permitted in their lives.

In the Garden of Olives He asked that the chalice of suffering pass from Him, and three times the answer was negative. He wanted to show us that suffering does not come into our lives without the permission or Will of the Father.

Jesus knew suffering would not pass from any of us after His Resurrection and He made sure we understood its role in our lives. Throughout the Gospels He promises us suffering and persecution, and He asks that we accept it with Joy.

He called all those who suffer "blessed" when they overcame their natural weaknesses. He promised Heaven to those who suffered interior and exterior poverty. To those who preferred God to themselves He promised Union with the Father.

To those who put their feelings and resentments aside and forgave, He promised Mercy. To those who struggled to maintain peace He promised sonship. And to those who suffered because they loved Him, He promised Joy.

Before all these fruits would be manifest, some kind of suffering was necessary. His own suffering would have been powerful enough to destroy suffering from the face of the earth, but He did not choose this course. He preferred to continue permitting suffering and make Himself the example for all men to follow.

He made it clear that suffering would be part of our lives when He said, "Come to Me, all you who labour and are overburdened and I will give you rest." He then explained why we should accept the burden of work and injustice, by adding that our crosses were really His Cross—His burden. "Shoulder My yoke and learn from Me, for I am gentle and humble of heart."

We are not to be without pain. Pain is Jesus suffering in us, but we are to look to Him for strength and courage. We are to learn this ability to shoulder our cross by gazing at Him and being gentle and humble in heart.

When we are gentle our crosses do not anger us or cause us to rebel. When we are humble we lovingly accept whatever the Father sends us. We see His pruning hand in everything we do or suffer. Only when we accept the sufferings in our lives with gentleness and humility will we be the recipients of the reward to follow — "You will find rest for your souls." Lest we forget that our sufferings come from Him, He said, "Yes, My yoke is easy and My burden light" (Matt. 11:28-30).

When we keep our eyes on Jesus, our sufferings are easier to bear. The realization that nothing happens to us that is not good for our souls, and that in reality He also suffers what we suffer, makes the yoke of pain a light burden.

A yoke placed between two oxen kept each one from going his own way. Yoked together, the load was easier to carry and the will of the farmer fulfilled. Jesus used the word "yoke" because when He places the burden of the cross upon our shoulders, He Himself shares the load. He has a definite plan in mind, a purification in view — one that is necessary if we are to live with Him in the Kingdom.

We do not know what fruit the Divine Gardener desires to harvest, but we may be sure that with the Providence of the Father behind us, and His Son beside us, and His Spirit within us, our share of the burden is small indeed.

St. Mark tells us that Jesus told His disciples one day "that the Son of Man was destined to suffer grievously." He was to be rejected and put to death. Peter's human nature rebelled at the thought of suffering, and believing Jesus to be Lord he desired that He use His Power and change this course of events.

Like all of us, Peter felt God should change man's free will and forever obliterate suffering from the world. Jesus rebuked Peter severely and said, "Get behind me, Satan! Because the way you think is not God's way but man's" (Mk. 8:31-33).

There are not many of us today who think in God's way. We think very much the way the world thinks of suffering.

There are many kinds of suffering that we can alleviate — sickness, inner resentments, injustice, and other evils. However, with all our compassion and intellectual astuteness in lessening pain, we are still overburdened with suffering in some form or other.

After Peter's cowardly statement, Jesus turned to His disciples and the people and said, "If anyone wants to be a follower of mine, let him renounce himself and take up his cross and follow me." In renouncing ourselves we must put aside our own ideas of how things should be and humbly accept the things we cannot change.

The acceptance of the cross is *the* condition of following Jesus. We are so concerned with our daily lives, our bodies, and our pleasures that the thought of mortification, suffering, pain, and penance makes us cry out in despair and discouragement.

This constant preoccupation with ourselves was criticized by Jesus. "Anyone who wants to save his life will lose it; but anyone who loses his life for My sake and for the sake of the Gospel, will save it" (Mk. 8:34-35). We shrink from suffering in any form. We desire to protect ourselves completely from pain, disappointment, and even death.

But Jesus reminds us that if we possess the whole world and lose eternal life it is a sad exchange. We think that gaining the whole world would be a blessing indeed, and yet Jesus expects us to be willing to give it up entirely for His sake, to count it as nothing.

Human nature desires comfort, security, unbounded happiness, perfect peace, and harmony. We prefer leisure to work and take the line of least resistance in any decision.

Jesus asks that we impose some suffering upon ourselves. He asks us to lay aside resentment and to love our enemies. He asks that we:

- give alms and not tell anyone of our good deeds.
- conquer our thoughts.
- be humble when we feel slighted.

- be content with the bread of today.
- fast and be cheerful.
- store up treasures only in Heaven.
- have complete trust in God and not in ourselves.
- see only our own faults and consider our neighbor's frailties as slight.
- not judge anyone.
- not swear or curse.
- have faith to move mountains.
- give up everything for His sake.

These counsels and many like them entail self-imposed suffering, sacrifice, and penance. Christianity is truly for the strong and courageous. It is not a pietistic balm for the consciences of men.

One day Jesus said to an astonished crowd: "Do you suppose that I have come to bring peace to the earth; it is not peace I have come to bring, but a sword." He then explained how children would be set against parents and parents against children (Matt. 10:34-36). This kind of dissension would be inevitable because Jesus required a total dedication of self to Him. So many people and so many things make demands upon us that giving ourselves to God completely causes cries of outrage to rise from friend and foe.

Lest we take His words as symbolic, Jesus added, "Anyone who prefers father or mother to Me is not worthy of Me. Anyone who prefers son or daughter to Me is not worthy of Me" (Matt. 10:37).

In order to cover every other area of sacrifice, be it house, land, or possessions, He told them, "Anyone who does not take his cross and follow in My footsteps is not worthy of Me" (Matt. 10:38).

The Cross Jesus carried all His life was hewn for Him by injustice, the greed of the ambitious, the selfishness of evil men, and the hatred of those in power. Even those who followed Him and considered themselves His friends were often a disappointment. But He did not rebel; He harbored no resentment.

He saw everything as the Father's Will, and in the Garden of Olives He stressed the Father's Will as the basis of His Sacrifice. The Father did not prevent those evil men from venting their wrath on His Son. Though He did not ordain their actions, He did permit them and used their malice for a greater good.

Jesus wanted us all to know that He could call on Legions of Angels to assist Him, but He would not. He was making a path for all of us to walk in, and that blood-stained road would lead us all to His Father.

Walking in His Footsteps

There can be no question in the mind of any Christian that his Savior was a Man of Sorrows. He has told us that He is the "way, the truth and the life" (Jn. 14:6). He entreated us to follow in His footsteps (Matt. 16:24) and to imitate His humility and meekness (Matt. 11:29).

To follow is to travel the same way a leader guides us. To imitate is to be like. When He gave Himself as Director and Direction on the path of Holiness, He also gave us a life filled with examples of how to act and react to every possible trial or heartache.

He promised us Joy but not without persecution. He promised a hundredfold but only after we had left all things for His sake.

He said we were *in* the world but not *of* it, and then He told us to go out and be a light to others.

When He warned us about being brought before judges and magistrates; He said we were not to worry about what we were to say. We were not to plan an argument beforehand. Our trust was to encompass everything from preaching the Good News to obtaining our daily bread.

He told us that He only said what He heard the Father say and only did what He saw the Father do. His entire life was lived in such a way that in following Him we might do as He did and think as He thought.

He promised His Apostles that they would want for nothing but warned them that they, too, would drink of the same chalice of which He drank and be baptized in the same suffering in which He was baptized.

In times of fear and anguish He asked His Apostles why they were agitated, and then proceeded to foretell greater sufferings to come.

He permitted Saul to bring to prison and death many Christians, and then knocked him off his horse and commissioned him to convert the Gentiles. As proof of His Authenticity, Jesus told Ananias, "I will show Paul what he will suffer for My sake" (Acts 9:16).

The reality of Paul suffering for the sake of Jesus was proof to Paul and the world that Jesus was truly the Lord.

Paul accepted this proof when he told the Christians "we prove we are God's servants by great fortitude in times of suffering" (2 Cor. 6:4). Here was a man who hated Jesus so much, he made others suffer for His Name. Suddenly, he changes and himself begins to suffer for that Name. His Christian career began with suffering as he fell from his horse and went blind, and ended with suffering at his death when he was beheaded at the command of Nero.

The world learned of Paul's love for Jesus by what he said and wrote, but that love was proved by what he *suffered*.

Our human nature is thrilled when love is expressed to us, but if that love fails in time of need or sacrifice, the beautiful words cherished before fall dead on our ears. Paul compared such love to clashing cymbals whose sound is deafening and painful.

Like a picture that speaks a thousand words, our willingness to suffer whatever He permits in our lives speaks an inaudible language that says, "I love Jesus." Our confidence in time of doubt says, "I trust Jesus." Our serenity in times of heartache says, "I believe in Jesus."

If we were both deaf and dumb, our union with God in times of trial would speak with such clarity that all men would know our love for Him was true.

There are those who say suffering is an evil because it is the result of evil men. Though Scripture tells us some men are "pregnant with mischief and bring forth lies" (Ps. 7:14), it also says if we persevere to the end in bearing injustice, as Jesus did, we shall be saved.

It is the desire of the Enemy to confuse our minds and harden our hearts against any kind of suffering for he knows the power it possesses before the Throne of God. We most resemble Jesus when we have the gift of suffering to offer with our prayers. It is not to our liking, but it is the vessel that bears our prayers to Heaven.

St. Paul told the Corinthians that "the language of the Cross may be illogical to those who are not on the way to salvation, but those of us who are on the way see it as God's power to save" (1 Cor. 1:18).

As the cross was a stumbling block to the Chosen People, it is so to many Christians. We look at suffering as *His* portion, not ours.

Times have not changed since the days of Paul, for we, too, demand miracles and signs, joy and happiness, health and prosperity, a guiltless conscience and unrepentant love. We want to think our journey should be sheer joy mixed with intermittent ecstasy.

Paul had the same problem with those who could not accept the reality that God used a Suffering Messiah to redeem them, "and so," he told the Corinthians, "while Jews demand miracles and the Greeks look for wisdom, here are we preaching a Crucified Christ; to the Jews an obstacle they cannot get over, to the pagans madness, but to those who have been called, whether they are Jews or Greeks, a Christ who is the Power and Wisdom of God. For God's foolishness is wiser than human wisdom and God's weakness is stronger than human strength" (1 Cor. 1:22-25).

We are forced to admit that even after two thousand years of Christianity, suffering is still "madness and an obstacle we cannot get over." It is to most, pure foolishness, but then how can human wisdom fathom the depths of God unless His own Spirit places some of the Divine Wisdom in our hearts so we no longer think the thoughts of men but of God?

Our reluctance to suffer for His sake adds burden to burden. Our arguments and resentments drag our cross along the path of life. Our make-believe world of Heaven here and Heaven there is a soap bubble silently drifting from one place to another, only to dissipate at the slightest touch.

As we go through life telling our neighbor there should be no suffering and telling ourselves we have no suffering, our time runs out and we are empty in heart and soul — weak members of a Body whose Head was crowned with Thorns.

Jesus said:

"In the world you will have trouble but be brave; I have conquered the world." (Jn. 16:33)

Paul told the Romans:

"I think that what we suffer in this life can never be compared to the glory, as yet unrevealed, which is waiting for us." (Rom. 8:18)

The writer of the Hebrews said:

"Suffering is part of your training; God is treating you as sons." (Heb. 12:7)

James said:

"My brothers, you will always have your trials but when they come try to treat them as a happy privilege." (Jas. 1:2)

Peter said:

"Think of what Christ suffered in this life and then arm yourselves with the same resolution that He had. Those whom God allows to suffer must trust themselves to the constancy of the Creator and go on doing good." (1 Pet. 4:1, 19)

And John said:

"We can be sure that we are in God only when the one who claims to be living in Him is living the same kind of life as Christ lived." (1 Jn. 2:5, 6)

You have read what Jesus, Peter, Paul, James, and John have said about suffering—and now:

What do you say?

His Pain — Like Mine

We often look at Jesus with an attitude of predestination — a cold, hard-hearted acceptance of His sufferings and pain. We think, at least in our subconscious, that somehow He *had* to do what He did, and so we slough it all off with a shrug of our shoulders, without a thought of the awesome wonder of a suffering God. We cannot comprehend a love that desires to *feel* our misery. The only love we understand is the kind that warms our heart and affects our emotions. We prefer that our love feels pity or sympathy, but not the actual pain of the one we love.

We may see someone with cancer, but we would never desire to actually feel every sharp, throbbing pain. We often say we would rather suffer than see those we love suffer, but this is, for the most part, a mere expression of sympathy.

Our meditations on His sufferings are shallow and distant — expressions of pity if we have any devotion or an acceptance of an historical fact that He came, suffered, and died.

We laboriously try to remember this reality during Lent and quickly forget it at Easter. We joyfully set aside His sufferings and don our Easter clothes as if to shed some disagreeable event by starting anew. Yes, the joy of His Resurrection should always be in our hearts and give us that hope that knows no sadness. But do we not lose the one element of Easter that assures our hope of a never-ending source of joy? "See My Hands and My Feet," Jesus told the doubting Thomas (see Lk. 24:39; Jn. 20:27). His risen, glorious body continues to carry wounds, but these wounds provide our greatest consolation, our deepest joy, and our assuring hope. These wounds open to us the secrets of His Love and give us a confident trust in His mercy. We can no longer doubt His love for us—we can no longer chide Him for permitting injustice in our lives while He never felt this painful sting.

Before redemption we may well have asked Him, "How do You know what it means to suffer, O God? Did You ever feel hungry or thirsty? Have Your nights ever been full of fears and Your days long hours of painful endurance? Have You ever felt lonely or rejected? Has anyone treated You unjustly, and have You ever cried? Has the powerful wind You created ever pierced Your bones and made You shiver with cold? Have you ever needed a friend and then, when he came along, watched him turn against You?"

His answer to all these questions would have been, "No." But now, we can no longer wonder, because His love has answered our unasked questions—has desired to *feel* what our nature *feels*, endure our weaknesses and limitations of our sinner condition, shouldered our yoke, and shuddered from the cold wind.

"The birds have nests and the foxes dens," He told His disciples, "but the Son of Man has nowhere to lay His Head" (Lk. 9:58). The realization that the love of Jesus shared and continues to share in our sorrows and pain, gives us that joy "no man can take away" (Jn. 16:22). Our continual Easter joy is mysteriously woven and interwoven with the cross.

The Christian experiences and lives a paradox. He possesses joy in sorrow, fulfillment in exile, light in darkness, peace in turmoil, consolation in dryness, contentment in pain, and hope in desolation. A dedicated Christian has the ability to take the present moment, look at it head on, recall the spirit of Jesus under similar circumstances and act accordingly. It is difficult, but He told us it would be, for the happiness He promised is beyond this life. We are given the opportunity to condition ourselves to live forever with Holiness Itself. Let us see how our daily lives and the life of Jesus parallel. Perhaps then it will be easier to change our lives accordingly.

In St. Matthew's Gospel we read that Jesus healed two demoniacs. These two men were possessed by demons who begged Jesus to let them go into a herd of pigs rather than into hell—their eternal home, and Jesus permitted them to go. The swineherds were so shocked, they ran into town to complain to the townspeople over the loss of their pigs. We see a strange reaction from the people—a reaction that baffles the mind and causes Jesus much pain. Scripture tells us that these two men were fierce, violent men who were a constant source of fear to all the people. The people's reaction to the healing should have been one of gratitude and love. However, we read, "that whole town set out to meet Jesus and as soon as they saw Him they implored Him to leave the neighborhood" (Matt. 8:34). They preferred their pigs to Jesus. They preferred that everything remain as it was if changing it cost them something. They were afraid of seeing Divine Power at work. It meant giving up their selfish ways, and they preferred that God leave them alone.

There are many occasions in the lifetime of a Christian when acts of love and sacrifice are not appreciated—when the aged are made to feel they are in the way and when loved ones make one feel unwanted. When these occasions arise, the soul should relate that feeling to the deep hurt in the Heart of Jesus as He was told to go away. He felt as we do—hurt and crushed—and He desires us to unite our pain to His and give it to the Father for the salvation of souls.

Prisoners too can relate to this incident in the life of Jesus in a special way. The two men who had been delivered from so many demons were ready to enter society once more. They had paid dearly for their indulgence, they had suffered from lack of dignity and respect and a total loss of hope. Yet the joy they expected from the crowd was lacking. No one was impressed by their conversion. There were only complaints over the cost of that conversion. The two men delivered by Jesus were delivered of violent, hateful demons, but were not the townspeople under the influence of the quiet demons of greed, ambition, self-indulgence, and selfishness? We cannot imagine the state of each soul who pleaded that God's Son leave their town. It is ironic that the two who were so visibly possessed were freed by the power of Jesus and accepted His love, while those who were respected citizens asked the God of Mercy to leave them alone.

Can it be that we are all in a kind of prison? Is it possible that those who are in prison today, publicly punished for their violence and crimes, have the opportunity to change and turn to Jesus, accept His Love, and end up more free in heart and soul than those outside prison walls?

Repentance can make the rejected ones acceptable to God, while pride makes those accepted by the world and its standards, rejected by God. When we begin to build walls of prejudice, hatred, pride, and self-indulgence around ourselves, we are more surely imprisoned than any prisoner behind concrete walls and iron bars. There are many imprisoned in this way for their entire lives — they never experience the freedom of the children of light, only the comfort of the false protection of the darkness. The pain of changing frightens them, and so they prefer their selfishness and complacency to the Word of God or the healing power of His Cross.

❧

One of the most frustrating sufferings Jesus bore must have been misunderstanding — a lack of comprehension on the part of those who loved Him and a lack of acceptance on the part of the authorities. A suffering Savior was not acceptable to either. A spiritual leader who spent time changing souls instead of governments had no place in their regime. He knew what they really needed to enter His Father's Kingdom, but they were interested in the kingdom of this world. They called it living a reality; He called it death. They thought of this life as the only one; He said it was only a place of exile while we waited for something greater. He told them the poor were blessed, and it was better to be virtuous than to gain the whole world; but to them worldly glory was too much to pass by for some invisible reality.

His Apostles were slow to understand the simplest parables, and often they would ask Him for explanations after the crowds were gone. He tried so hard to bring the Mystery of the Father's Love down to the language of children, but even that was often beyond the reach of His disciples — the men destined to go and preach the Good News to everyone. He would often look at them with amazement and say, "Do you not understand either?" (Mk. 7:18). Even His miracles were misunderstood, His authority questioned, and His relatives sought Him out as some madman. His discernment was questioned because He permitted a sinner to touch Him and His reputation held in suspicion because He ate with sinners. When He healed on the Sabbath, He was a lawbreaker and when He demanded love as the most important Commandment, He was labeled an innovator.

There are hardly any human beings who have not felt this pain of misunderstanding in their lives in some form or other. Our motives are rashly judged, or our virtue is called hypocrisy. Our ideas are too bold or our caution called timidity. Children accuse parents of interference when loving correction warns of danger. We're tagged fanatics if Jesus is a part of our daily living, but when tragedy strikes, Job's comforters confront us with our lack of piety as God's vengeance strikes us for some hidden resentment that must be lurking in our hearts. When we're compassionate towards sinners, we're accused of imprudence, and when just anger makes us lash out, we are called uncharitable. The list of the incongruities could be multiplied a hundredfold, and the more we try to make them right, the more entangled we become. But we can always look at Jesus and know He understands. Like Him, we can do the Father's Will according to the light we have and be at peace. His sufferings formed part of our redemption; ours form part of our sanctification.

"It began to blow a gale and the waves were breaking into the boat so that it was almost swamped. But He [Jesus] was in the stern, His head on a cushion, asleep" (Mk. 4:37-38).

The all-powerful God, out of whose Hands planets and galaxies tumbled, became a man and was tired! He had reached a point of physical exhaustion that neither rain, nor wind, nor the shouts of fear-gripped men could overcome. He was dead tired—every muscle, every bone, every nerve had reached the end of its endurance, and sleep alone would bring back that energy so necessary for the human body to function well.

We have all felt tired—tired from work and often tired *of* work. We all reach a time when we must stop and rest. It is at this time we can relate to Jesus in a very conscious way. He and we know what it means to be worn out. We can unite our fatigue with His and offer it to the Father as a holocaust of love and obedience. Our work, our mission, and our state of life accomplished according to His holy Will make common fatigue a channel of grace and power. It becomes more than the natural consequence of exertion; it becomes a sacrifice of praise, an act of penance, a personal holocaust of love.

"An hour later another man insisted saying, 'This fellow was certainly with Him. Why, he is a Galilean.' 'My friend,' said Peter, 'I do not know what you are talking about.' At that instant ... the cock crowed and the Lord turned and looked straight at Peter" (Lk. 22:59-61). We have a tendency to get caught up in Peter's denial in this Scripture passage. But have we thought of Jesus? Jesus heard Peter call a perfect stranger "friend" and then go on to deny the only true friend he possessed—Jesus. The Heart of Jesus was surely crushed. Those who arrested Him hated Him, and although His Heart was deeply hurt, imagine the searing throb of pain as He heard with His own ears the rejection of His Love by a friend.

Peter was the man He had loved much, given much to, and depended upon to carry His message of love to the world. Here He heard him deny he even knew the One he was to represent on earth. Can any of us plumb the depths of disappointment and pain in the soul of Jesus? Perhaps we can, perhaps all men can at one time or another. Parents are hurt over children who flippantly throw away their care, advice, love, and protection. Children too, whose hearts cry out for love, often see parents running after the things that perish and having little concern for the souls God has entrusted to their care as parents. Friendship too can suffer a mortal blow when one party yields to suspicion, distrust, jealousy, or misunderstanding. Yes, all of us can relate in some way to the deep hurt in the Heart of Jesus as He heard His friend and companion deny knowing Him. Let us unite our pain to His and give it to the Father for the salvation of souls, when we experience the rejection of a loved one.

❧

"John came, neither eating nor drinking and they say, 'He is possessed.' The Son of Man came, eating and drinking, and they say, 'Look, a glutton and a drunkard, a friend of tax collectors and sinners'" (Matt. 11:18-19). No matter what God did, those in authority were never satisfied. He sent His prophet John, a man of great penance, frugal, ascetical, and demanding. His penitential spirit pricked their consciences so they condemned Him. Jesus came as one who was kind, gentle, merciful, and they called Him names to make Him look small and of no consequence.

John appealed to the ninety-nine and called them to repentance, while Jesus went after the stray sheep. Both, however, were unacceptable. Some men desire knowledge with which to speculate, but not Spirit-filled words that stir the heart and cause them to change.

No matter what Jesus did, someone found fault with it. When His anger raged at the money changers in the temple, they questioned His authority to take matters into His own hands. When His compassion reached out in mercy to the adulteress, they questioned His courage. No wonder He told His Apostles that the opinions of men meant nothing to Him (Jn. 5:41). It is also true with us for there are times when our best actions and purest motives are held in question. There are times we bend over backward to please, but to no avail. When this happens we must look at Jesus and do as He did—He accomplished the Will of God in the present moment, and regardless of public reaction, He went His way in peace. He had come to save men, not to conduct an opinion poll. It was only important to Him that He did what He saw the Father do and said what He heard the Father say. He was the perfect image of the Father, and that Image turned some against Him and drew others to Him. The choice was theirs; their wills were free. He offered them love because He was Love Itself, but His peace was not dependent upon their acceptance. His love was deep enough to continue loving them and powerful enough to remain at peace when they preferred themselves to Him. His love enveloped everyone; it was they who left the radius of that love.

We see this in the rich young man. Scripture tells us he ran up to Jesus and "knelt before Him." He wanted to inherit eternal life and asked Jesus how to do it. Jesus told him to keep the commandments, but the young man found that rather easy. He had formed the habit of keeping the law. He wanted more—his soul somehow knew there was something better. Jesus "looked at him steadily and loved him," the passage continues, but then the blow came. The great challenge was given. "Go and sell everything you own and give the money to the poor and you will have treasure in heaven; then come, follow me" (Mk. 10:17-22). Immediately, the enormity of the challenge struck the young man like a bolt of lightning. He had not expected that answer to his question; he was not ready for the sacrifice.

Jesus knew what the young man would have to give up, but He also knew what glory and renown he would miss for all eternity by passing up the opportunity of following Him. The young man thought he possessed too much to give up; he did not realize he gave up more than he possessed by not following the call of Jesus. It is often so with us. We know what people are doing to their immortal souls when they insist on seeking the things that pass, when a dissolute life is the order of the day, when they seemingly cannot tear themselves away from a life of sin. Their excuse is that they cannot give up their weaknesses, and yet they do not understand what they really are giving up. The paradox is in the sad reality that they cannot give up misery, but they are capable of giving up eternal joy!

How truly we can say that He understands our pains and heartaches: His pain was like mine. Thank you, Jesus, for loving us all so much!

BURNOUT

Dawn on the Mountain: The Gift of Dryness in Prayer

※

"A Sacred Way" (Isa. 35:8)

Every Christian who strives for holiness of life experiences dryness of soul. It is to most people a heartrending experience. It is a paradox, for the soul becomes confused when it realizes the harder it strives, the further away Jesus seems to be.

How strange is a spiritual life that draws a soul to a fire only to make it feel freezing cold! It is, to all appearances, a contradiction. In the world, the closer we are to a friend or loved one, the more secure and unafraid we become. The deeper the love, the more glowing one feels in the presence of the beloved. And so it is as we grow in the love of God. He wants us to love Him "in Spirit and in Truth," and this kind of love is above human love—as much above as is the difference between the flicker of a match and the noonday sun.

Human love in all its beauty and warmth must be raised to a level above itself. The air at the foot of a high mountain is easier to breathe, even though it is not as pure as the air on the summit. To breathe that pure air, our bodies would have to adapt themselves to the atmosphere of the mountain peak. The peace and quiet and the view from that height are well worth the effort and the pain of climbing.

We would, however, encounter one phenomenon during our climb and that is a certain kind of loneliness. The further up the mountain we travel, the fewer companions we have. There comes a time when all things seem to drop behind and we find ourselves alone. When we finally arrive on the top the loneliness is gone, for we see things very differently. We see all our former companions and possessions as they really are, with no illusions, no regrets, and no attachments. In this rare air of God's Love we possess Wisdom, which is the Word of God—Jesus. We see things as He sees them because the breath of His Spirit fills our souls to overflowing.

To those who live in the sunshine of the valley, our life atop the mountain is forever dull and lonely, but it is only because they do not share the view. Sometimes we come down the mountain and bask in the sunshine, but soon we must ascend again and fill our souls with the fresh air of His Love.

This is but a faint picture of dryness of soul and the beautiful work it accomplishes. There are times in life when God seems very close. The sun of His Love shines brightly. Our hearts exult and our being is rapt in the joy of His Presence. There are other times, however, when His Presence fades away like a morning mist and we find ourselves shivering from the cold. Though the whole world were to love and applaud us it would all be as nothing, for the sunshine of our life—God—seems gone, and our soul cannot be consoled except by Him.

We wander from place to place looking for Him; we try to pray, to meditate on His life, to imitate His virtues, but nothing seems to alleviate the emptiness in the depths of our being. Our life goes on, and we work, eat, sleep, laugh, and cry but none of these functions fill the void.

There is a longing for God that does not seem to be satisfied by anything or anyone. A darkness descends, but in it we do not sleep or feel refreshed. It is a darkness that keeps us ever awake—ever looking—ever yearning for the dawn.

It is a thirst that is never quenched, for every drop of "living water" makes us thirst for more. Days, months, and years can be spent in this state of dryness. Sometimes doubts as to the very existence of God surround the soul with their icy embrace, and the blackest midnight descends and fills the soul with emptiness.

Though our poor human nature rebels at this state of soul, it realizes that somehow great work is being accomplished. The silent Hand of God moves on, purifying the faculties of our soul, detaching us from possessions, people, and ourselves, raising us to various heights of prayer, and increasing our capacity for love.

This dryness is like a spiritual anesthetic. It numbs our soul while the Master Sculptor shapes it into His Image. We have no feeling of anything being accomplished. It is as if we were suspended between heaven and earth. We desire nothing of this world, but we are still not ready for the pure air on the mountain of God. We wait, not always patiently, while we roam along unknown paths, thinking at times we are lost, but always finding a new path to take, a new cave to hide in, a dim light to follow.

God speaks to our souls, but we are so busy looking for Him we do not near His Voice. We are desolate and become aggravated with ourselves and others. Not possessing the humility to realize we can do nothing of ourselves, we become feverishly active, perform more good works, read books, and distract ourselves from the emptiness that fills our souls.

Without realizing it, we are actually running away from the fire and into the cold, dark night. Our souls are restless for the warmth of His Love, and we do all we can to bring back past consolations. Our Memory serves us well by recalling what used to be, and we look back with great longing, convinced that somehow we are being chastised for some weakness or frailty.

This is not to say that dryness is not caused by lukewarmness, because it often is, but we must examine ourselves to judge the cause. We cannot torment our souls with scruples and doubts.

If our dry spell causes us pain, increases our thirst for God, makes us strive for virtue, and during prayer makes every other thought outside of God distasteful to us, then we can assume that the dryness we experience is of God. God is calling us to a higher form of prayer and a deeper union with Himself.

Those who are lukewarm do not miss His Presence; they do not imitate His virtues, and their prayer time, if any, is spent in willful distractions geared towards their own pleasure and convenience. For these souls we pray. We ask God for the grace of perseverance for ourselves so we do not fall away from His Love and Mercy.

In order to better understand the power and beauty of spiritual dryness, we will look at its various aspects and try to reap the fruit of this call to greater things.

Dryness of the Mind

"See where He stands, behind our wall. He looks in at the window, He peers through the lattice" (Songs 2:9).

In the beginning of our spiritual life God floods our souls with consolations, but before long His Love demands that we rise above the feeling level and adore Him "in spirit and truth" (Jn. 4:23, 24).

So begins a kind of hide-and-seek. As the Sacred writer records, God stands "behind a wall" blocked from our view, but He often "peers through the window" to give us a glimpse of His beautiful Face. At other times it is as if a "lattice" were between the soul and God; we see Him and yet we do not.

In this state of finding yet not finding, the soul is content with at least a little consolation. It becomes aware of His

Presence even though that Presence is obscured by the things of this world and the frailties of human nature.

In the past, meditations were a sheer joy, and the soul believed that it had arrived at perfect peace. Its passions were in control, and prayer was a glorious experience.

It is easy to be virtuous under these conditions. God lifts us out of ourselves and carries us along with ease. Our inner selves, enjoying the consolations of God, are so rapt in the sweetness of His Presence that there is little chance of a permanent change. The Presence of all Goodness is like a magnet drawing us to Himself; our weaknesses and passions are not gone, only dormant. They sleep while we are free to roam the realms of love in peace.

This state of soul cannot last for long. We have been given the grace to participate in the very nature of God. To fulfill this God-given role we must become more and more like Him. We cannot do this if we inordinately cling to the emotions of our human nature.

In our daily life, human love rests for the most part on a sense level, but since God is Spirit we must communicate with Him on a spirit-to-spirit level. We must be detached from the world and ourselves and seek Him for Himself alone. It is for this purpose that Jesus tells us "every branch that does bear fruit the Father prunes to make it bear more fruit" (Jn. 15:2). It is those who are putting forth great effort to become like Jesus that God plunges into the darkness of dryness and into an awareness of their imperfections. So begins the purification of our faculties—Memory, Understanding, and Will—and the beginning of our ascent to the Mountain of Holiness.

The faculty that is of great help in our meditations is our Memory. It can recall incidents in the life of Jesus and picture them to our minds and make meditation a sheer delight. It is easy to recall Jesus in the Agony in the Garden and imagine ourselves kneeling beside Him and consoling Him in His hour of need. We may be content to lovingly look at Him in His fear and feel His pain.

Our Memory can serve us in a beautiful way during a meditation by bringing back the words of Jesus, His gestures, and His beautiful Face. This use of Memory and Imagination can be of tremendous help by giving us a strong motive for following Jesus. It can fire us with zeal for His Glory and inspire us to work for the salvation of souls.

The Memory excites our emotions and our senses. Both virtue and sin can find a home in our Memory and drive us to sanctity or damnation. Our five senses, prodded on by our Reason, can lead us to heroic deeds of valor or black despair. Our Wills, strong and powerful, can become so weak that we are "reeds shaken by the wind" (see Lk. 7:24).

In a state of dryness, however, God purifies all three of these faculties in order to raise them up to the level of Jesus. When Paul asked us to "put on the mind of Christ" (1 Cor. 2:16) he was speaking of a purification initiated by God that raised our faculties to a spiritual plane. This purification is one we must accept, endure, and courageously persevere in as long as God wills it.

The first faculty to feel the pruning of the Father is our Memory. It is as if all things good and holy were blanked out of our minds. We not only find Meditation impossible but even distasteful.

We endure this state for a few days, thinking it will pass as all other trials do, but when the days pass on to weeks and months, sometimes into years, our Intellect tells us we are wasting our time.

It is at this state of soul that the evil spirits, who realize the importance of dryness, tempt us to give up prayer, or torture us with the thought that some past sin has incurred God's anger upon us and He has left us to our miserable selves.

Only the grace of God keeps us from despairing, for He gives us enough light and courage to continue praying despite the dryness inside and the assaults of the evil one outside.

Another phenomenon occurs in this state of soul, and that is an exaggerated view of our weaknesses, faults, and imperfections that we have long accepted and fought against; they become so big that they engulf our souls like a huge monster.

Those with whom we live or work become aggravating and unbearable. It is as if the whole world were determined to destroy us. Sometimes sickness besets us, and this, too, is borne with impatience and fear.

We are so engulfed in the pain of dryness and the avalanche of trials that we are under the impression we fight alone, unloved by God and distressed by our neighbors.

It is at this point that we "don't do the things we want to do and do the things we don't want to do" (see Rom. 7:19). What we fail to see is God's loving hand guiding us and leading us gently up the Mountain of Holiness. We feel so unholy, wicked, and lonely that God and His Kingdom are far removed from our hearts. There is such a difference between His Infinite Holiness and our poor distressed souls that all we feel is unclean.

Our Intellect, reasoning on a human level, keeps telling us that sanctity is not for us. It is obviously for those who have fortitude to accomplish great deeds and possess great talents and gifts.

As if to add fuel to the fire, our Wills begin to vacillate and are confused as to the course to take. Our ability to accomplish anything on a spiritual level is difficult. A "do nothing" attitude grips our souls, and lukewarmness tries to wrap its arms around us.

It is near impossible for the soul to see how any good could come from this state of mind. But if the soul perseveres in its prayers and acts of virtue in spite of how it feels, it will soon begin to realize that its purification is good, and freedom of spirit will be its reward.

Even though distractions plague its prayer time, the soul calmly returns to its seeking of the Lord as soon as those distractions are noticed. The danger here is for the soul to seek consolations by deliberate distractions. Meditative reading is put aside, and the soul spends the whole time of prayer reading a book that gives it consolation but little fervor. The shortening of prayer time is a real danger, for the fear of "wasting" time takes hold of the soul. It seeks more action, and soon the good works that bring consolation replace prayer time and the soul falls prey to great danger.

It is important to persevere in praying, even in lengthening the time of prayer, for the purification of dryness far outweighs the few consolations the soul derives from active works to distract it. To refuse to accept dryness is to refuse growth in the spiritual life. It is the vertical beam of our daily cross.

This is not to say that everyone suffers from dryness in the same way or for the same length of time. Some souls suffer little from this type of purification, and God can and often does lead them to great sanctity.

Jesus compared the Spirit to a wind when He spoke to Nicodemus, "Do not be surprised when I say, 'You must be born from above.' The wind blows wherever it pleases; you hear its sound but you cannot tell where it comes from or where it is going. That is how it is with all who are born of the Spirit" (Jn. 3:7-8). The Sanctifier of our souls leads each one in a different way. It is not our duty to question how or why. We need only to trust His guidance of our souls, and if "dryness" is our constant companion, it is our way—the way of Faith—of Trust—of Love.

Dryness sharpens every faculty. It forces us to great degrees of Hope when our Memory and Imagination are dulled. It increases our Faith, for we must seek Him as He is and believe His Word. It strengthens our Will by making it follow His Commandments and imitate His virtues.

Our faculties seek this Lord as a deer seeks running water and they constantly look out for Him in an effort to find Him. "Have you seen Him whom my heart loves?" (Songs 3:3), the soul repeats over and over as it does all in its power to find what it feels it has lost.

As the soul is not aware of the life-giving blood flowing through its body, neither is it aware of the life-giving grace increasing in itself through the quiet flow of dryness.

Detachment is one of the greatest works of dryness. It is great because it is detaching ourselves from ourselves and not from things. Things are comparatively easy to give up when we feel the loving arms of God around us. We are strangely very much aware of ourselves at this time. Though we enjoy the Presence of God, it is the joy we are experiencing that occupies our mind and heart. So conscious are we of our sweet feelings that the loss of consolation causes us great pain. A void is created, but how often that void is more an absence of ourselves from feelings rather than an absence from His Presence.

Our Faith tells us that God is always Present to us and by grace He is in our souls. Dryness then forces us to live by what Faith teaches rather than what our feelings make us desire. Unless God bestows upon us the searing power of dryness we shall forever be swayed by emotional feelings designed to prod us on but never capable of changing us.

How true is the passage from the Song of Songs, "Catch the foxes for us, the little foxes that make havoc of the vineyards, for our vineyards are in flower" (2:15). Truly the soul is ready to bloom in the Presence of its Creator, but first those attachments, imperfections, and weaknesses must be overcome. The soul must be free to live in the Presence of its Lord at all times. Its Memory must be calmed and controlled, its Intellect raised above itself in pure Faith, and its Will strong enough to follow in the footsteps of the Master.

How beautiful is the cross that brings about such marvelous changes in the soul. How grateful we should be to God for His patience with us even though we struggle against His Providence and Guidance. Let us not become giddy as we climb the Mountain of Holiness and forget our goals, our desires, and our way. If we ask God for sanctity we must believe that He has heard our prayer, and everything in our moment-to-moment existence is designed by Him for that end.

Jesus has promised that when the Father sees us bearing fruit He will prune us so we may bear more fruit. It is by dryness again that God purifies our hearts. Our love, like His, must be pure and unselfish. It is in this area that dryness does its most glorious work.

Dryness of the Heart

Although our minds find it difficult to pray or concentrate on spiritual things during aridity, it is bearable when we have at least some knowledge of the love God has for us.

Our striving to pray and practice virtue in the midst of dryness gives us some assurance that we do love God or we would not endure this trial.

And so it is that a knowledge of God's love for us and our love for Him becomes the strong rope that we cling to as we climb the Mountain of Holiness.

But one day this prop is also taken away, and our hearts are left without the least sign of love. The special assurance is gone, and we feel the cold wind of the heights. Only the elements remain to strengthen and purify our hearts of all self-indulgence and selfish love.

We are offered the opportunity to love God for Himself without expecting anything in return. We are given the chance of loving Him when there are no manifest gifts and no consolations to encourage us. We are bereft of any feeling of love, and the desire for this sweet gift wells up in our hearts, only to be disappointed by no response.

Now we stand alone before the Majesty of God, and the brightness of that light makes us recoil at the difference between us. We feel unloved and unloving. When dryness attacked our minds there was at least a shred of love residing in our hearts, but now that is gone and we are forced to love only because we want to.

We are so accustomed to love on a human level that we find loving God for Himself either impossible or beyond our capabilities. We tend to love those who appeal to us, render us a service, or are good to us. In the degree they perform these various services we love them.

We often say that this particular person is our best friend. Usually this means that the person has the same goals, ambitions, likes, and dislikes as we. This friend makes us feel at ease in his presence, and so we are fond of his company. What we most often like is the consolation afforded us. This is why in times of trial, sickness, or hardship, some friends drift apart and find each other boring.

However, a true friend loves us in every possible circumstance or trial. In fact, differences deepen our friendship because true love is fed by sacrifice.

Because God is spirit, invisible, and all-perfect, our relationship with Him is often built on the "Rich Uncle" concept that He has everything to give and we have only to receive. That we have anything to give upsets our theology and increases our responsibility. Any friendship not based on a mutual giving will not last. Selfish love cannot exist between friends for very long, and if that love is the basis of our relationship to God, it is a disaster. Yet to love on a selfish level is so basic to our nature. We tend to love Him on the same level as we love our neighbor—for what He does or can give us.

Dryness of heart—that purifying cross—cleanses our love of all selfishness and raises it to a level of unselfish love. We begin to love freely—because we want to—because God is all-lovable. The wrenching of self from our prayer time with God, by this inability to "feel" any love in our hearts, raises us to the level of the New Commandment. On this level of prayer, we pray and love God for Himself alone, not for the gifts or consolations He gives us. This new attitude and degree of love extends itself to our neighbor, and we begin to love him in the same way God loves us—unselfishly.

Only through the pain of dryness—where we decrease and He increases—can we begin to love God in the way He wishes us to love. When we pray we are doing so on our will power, for our poor human nature receives no compensation for its efforts.

Faith tells us that God is present when we pray, and Hope tells us He listens, but only Love makes us continue to pray when darkness, boredom, and even disgust fill our souls to overflowing. Only a true love will persevere in praying despite darkness and confusion.

Must God try us so? Yes, because He wants us to love as He loves and be holy as He is holy. Through His Grace, His Presence, and His Love in our souls He cries out for us to love Him as He is and to be so attuned to His Spirit that the mere whisper of His Voice enkindles our hearts with love.

This is difficult for our human nature to understand. Human love is associated with feelings, such as the feeling of benevolence, the feeling of confidence, the feeling of filial or paternal love, the love born of friendship, and the love that makes a man and woman desire to live together in a State of Marriage. All these kinds of love are connected in various ways to feelings, and so it is natural for us to think that our love for God should be on the same level.

This conviction is strengthened by the fact that when we first found the Lord we experienced a tremendous emotional uplift. Our hearts sang the praises of God with great enthusiasm. We bore pain with joy, and if misfortune overtook us we accepted it with a flare of detachment that was never experienced before.

When God began to prune that which was so good in the beginning, it was natural to think consolations would continue. We expected to work hard and give up much—but the fire of His Love, so sweet to our taste, would never leave us.

The knowledge that His Presence never leaves us adds to the cross of dryness because we think that Presence must be felt. We are slow to understand that God wants us to have both a yearning and an assurance of His Presence—but in Faith. His Presence dwelling in our hearts increases our capacity for love. His Grace, ever gratuitous and independent of our good actions, increases our degree of love and permits us to return love for love. His love in us—as we are emptied of self—becomes our love for Him. We begin to love Him with the love of the Spirit ever dwelling in our hearts.

Through the purification of dryness of heart, the Holy Spirit becomes the greatest love in our souls. We begin to love God with our Will. We choose to love Him, to spend some time with Him, to prefer Him to ourselves. It is a hard lesson to learn, but God slowly guides our poor hearts towards Himself and frees us of all the attachments that keep us from giving ourselves to Him totally.

Dryness takes away the wrong kind of love in our hearts and leaves the heart empty and ready for a Divine influx of Grace—a greater participation in the Divine Nature—a purer, unadulterated love—a love that is God Himself.

Like all operations, this is extremely painful because it strikes at the very source of "feelings," consolations, and the sense of well-being that we call happiness. It cuts deep into our selfish love and ruthlessly carves it out. It is when we gaze up to the Father in anguish of heart, lonely and empty, that the Spirit of Love accepts the ashes of our human love and begins His work of transformation. It is time for Jesus to bear fruit in our souls.

Dryness Leads to Detachment

Perhaps one of the first fruits the Spirit bears in our souls through the purification of dryness is detachment.

The people and things we are attached to are the things we love selfishly. We find comfort and consolation in them, and in proportion as our souls cling to these feelings, in that proportion we are attached.

Attachments to spiritual experiences lead to spiritual gluttony. We seek consolations, become disconsolate without them, jealous of those who possess them, and are never satisfied with God's plan in our lives. We demand from God or bring upon ourselves consolations, the fruit of which is a repugnance for suffering in any form. We run from the pruning hand of the Father, and in so doing deprive our souls of the consolations at the heights of prayer. We are not willing to give up the sweetness of being aware of the Presence of God for the growth of Faith in our lives.

This unwanted and unappreciated dryness of soul brings about the virtue we do not have the courage to exercise — detachment. It has the power to strip us of the things we desire and covet most of all — feelings. By the stripping down of feelings, dryness leaves our souls open to objective thinking, clear thinking, and an unselfish concern for others.

If we are patient with our dryness, we will see clearly how it separates our personal feelings from prayer and various incidents of daily life. The constant demand made upon us during prayer habituates us to unselfish living.

If we are strong enough to love and commune with God, without feelings, we shall do the same with our neighbor. We shall love that neighbor with a detached love. This means we make loving more important than being loved in return.

The soul realizes that in this short journey of life, it has the opportunity to manifest its love for Jesus by comforting Him, being zealous for His Glory rather than its own, and growing in that God-like love whose seed was planted in the soul at Baptism.

This is the time to console Jesus by a perfect union of our will with His—a loving acceptance of the work of His Spirit in our souls.

There are so many things in life to which we become attached. We are encouraged by the world to possess as many things as possible. The concept of poverty of spirit is foreign and unacceptable to the world, and it is abhorrent to the demons.

It is necessary then for God to place us in a position of detachment—a kind of involuntary renunciation—that will prune our souls and lead them to freedom. We are slow to detach ourselves, and when we manage some kind of voluntary detachment, we begin by doing without the things we care for the least. Those things dear to our hearts we rationalize into keeping, or we leave them till last.

The Spirit of God assists us in this painful mortification by giving us a dryness of soul that does not find pleasure or comfort in anything. Even nature, beautiful and majestic as it comes from the Power of God, leaves us cold and unimpressed.

The love of friends only makes us realize how much we miss His Presence. The thought of past spiritual experiences, when we were aware of His Love and Goodness, only creates a greater void that nothing can fill.

The more we reach out to creatures to fill the void in our hearts, the deeper that void becomes. Like the Bride in the Song of Songs, we cry out to everyone, "Have you seen Him whom my heart loves?" (Songs 3:3). What a blessing that God's pruning does not permit us to find comfort in anyone or anything. Surely, we would cling to the least comfort and be willing to forego our climb up the Mountain of Holiness if we could find solace in creation.

We are so caught up in our own miseries that our soul becomes very much aware of itself. Like bodily pain, when the mind focuses itself almost entirely on one small part of the body, the soul becomes painfully aware of its finiteness and its total inability to accomplish any good work on its own. Now it is that it becomes detached from the desire for consolation. The sight of its limitations forces the soul to depend entirely upon God and His Grace to bear fruit. It has begun to realize that without Him it "can do nothing" (Jn. 15:5).

It is important at this stage for the soul to possess a healthy self-love. If it does not, the consciousness of its imperfections, weaknesses, and frailties, plus the dryness, will bring the soul to near despair. By "healthy" self-love is meant a realization of the soul's value and uniqueness before God. So much is the individual soul loved by the Father, that He gave His only Son for its salvation and eternal happiness. It must understand and make a distinction then between who it is and what it does.

The weaknesses it is guilty of can be changed and transformed by the love of Jesus and the grace of His Spirit. The realization of the dignity of the soul after Baptism must never be smothered under the frailties of its nature. The individual is a child of God, an heir to the Kingdom, and the thought of God's Infinite Mercy in its regard must ever keep the soul elevated above itself.

If we cannot love ourselves as a masterpiece of God's Power and at the same time hate the sins we commit, we shall be unable to relate to our neighbor in love. When we find sin we shall hate the sinner and fail to make the distinction between our neighbor and his weaknesses. It will be difficult to love that neighbor in the way God loves Him because that neighbor must be near perfect before he is the recipient of our love. The Commandment will be merely an ideal that is not realistic in modern-day living.

When we are detached from ourselves we suddenly find that loving our neighbor is easy. We no longer make distinctions between those we "like" and those we "love." The selfish motives that attracted us to some and repelled us from others, have been swallowed up in the chasm of our own nothingness. Jesus has filled the void created and sustained by dryness. His Love in our hearts reaches out to love everyone, while it sees material possessions as passing trinkets in time.

Dryness Leads to Humility

One of the most painful lessons that Dryness teaches us is the spirit of Humility. Our total helplessness in the face of our inability to pray can almost annihilate our pride. We may rebel against this feeling of inadequacy, but if we accept it we can make a giant stride towards a spirit of Humility.

The humility that is the fruit of dryness is not self-imposed, so the soul is guarded against a false humility which says it can do nothing of itself but does not really believe it. Neither is this humility the fruit of persecution or misunderstanding. It is, therefore, a safeguard against the resentment that often accompanies the clashes of personality traits in our relationship with others.

It is a crushing blow to our pride to realize we must wait upon the Lord to pray well or to pray at all. We often read and reread Jesus' statement that without Him we can do nothing but this hardly reaches an experimental stage in our lives. When we kneel before Him, helpless, dry, and in a state of confusion, we begin to "feel" our finite condition. A reality of life becomes an experience for us—it becomes a startling fact that without Him we can do nothing—not even pray.

It is good to have an intellectual awareness of our dependence upon God—to understand how great He is and how very small we are in His sight. But when our very bones feel the crushing weight of His Holiness upon us and we are conscious of our sinner condition, then we pass from knowing about God to knowing God, for the former is knowledge and the latter, experience.

Though the essence of dryness is a lack of feeling, the consciousness of one's unworthiness, with all the weaknesses of human nature strong and operative, is very much a "feeling" but one not to our liking. We try to run away from the feeling of our nothingness that overwhelms us, but we cannot. It is one of the many phenomena of the spiritual life that "no feeling" produces a "feeling." The soul's awareness of its wretched condition can do more to its pride in five minutes than a thousand humiliations in a lifetime.

Not only does the soul possess a new sense of its dependence upon God, but its self-knowledge is increased to an alarming degree. Every fault is magnified, and the soul sees weaknesses within it that never before came to the surface.

This self-knowledge is the very root of Humility, and when the soul sees itself as it really is and then gazes at the Infinite

God who loves it, the reality of the vast difference between them engenders Humility, provided that this knowledge is accepted with a deep sense of gratitude.

This gratitude is not only for the light given but for the gratuitous love bestowed upon the lowly soul by the Infinite God. The reality of God's personal love for a poor weak human being sends the soul into transports of joy, even though the feeling of dryness fills the soul with consternation and its weaknesses overwhelm it. In its very depths, there begins a quiet acceptance of itself and of God, and a determined effort evolves that drives the soul on to a deeper love in a spirit of sacrifice.

The soul slowly understands what humility of heart means. It does not feel crushed or broken, but it is overwhelmed by a "sense" of its sinner condition, of its capacity for evil, and the thin thread that separates it from God, whose "power is at its best in weakness" (2 Cor. 12:9).

It is no longer discouraged by its tendencies towards sin; it is more surprised at what it does not do, and implores the grace of God to ever stay in His favor. Its striving for perfection becomes more interior, and with the effort to overcome exterior faults it tries to improve its motives. It strives to be gentle not only in action but in heart.

There comes to the soul a realization that but for the grace of God it is capable of any sin. It therefore is more humble in its attitude towards the weak and more gentle if and when correction is necessary.

The inner conviction of the soul's capacity for evil, though it ever strives for holiness, prevents that arrogance that finds fault with others. Only the soul that "feels" it is nothing but keeps its eyes on Jesus can begin the climb up the mountain of perfection. The soul at this stage does not expect much of itself since its self-knowledge has been increased. It does expect much from God, however, because it realizes the real source of its power. And so the soul learns to harmonize self-knowledge that expects little good from itself, and Hope in God, from Whom it expects everything.

Dryness again becomes the pivot point for a balance of opposite emotions—deep repentance and great love, fear of the Lord and confidence, distrust of one's own strength and hope in His power, fear of one's own weaknesses and trust in His Grace.

Though failure, pain, and suffering humble our minds, it is the power of dryness that God uses to humble our hearts. Jesus warned us that it was from men's hearts that evil arose, and so it is our hearts that God purifies and humbles so that the seed of evil, sown by the enemy, may not take root.

Dryness Leads to Patience

One of the most difficult virtues for our human nature to acquire is Patience.

Patience is that ability to wait in peace.

There are few of us who possess Patience on a natural level, for our modern-day world has conditioned us to perform every duty in record time. We purchase whatever food is instant, and whatever mode of travel is the faster. Though we complain of boredom we are in a hurry to get anywhere we are going, and then we rush when we arrive so we can return in the shortest possible time.

We are "victims" of a hurried society—part of a perpetual merry-go-round that is constantly in motion but never leaves its place. Our feet run on an invisible treadmill that keeps us out of breath while we rush from one activity to another.

Loud music and clashing sounds keep our nerves frayed and our emotions at a high pitch. Like the voice of a circus barker crying, "Hurry, Hurry, Hurry," the world keeps us all in some kind of motion so we do not have time to think, pray, or otherwise get our wits together.

The Holy Spirit cannot work in this din and clamor. As Elijah realized—the Spirit is like a gentle breeze, quietly inspiring, and speaking softly in the silence of our hearts (see 1 Kgs. 19:12-13). Rushing, noise, uneasiness, lack of self-control, and the constant move towards more and more action, drown His Voice and nullify His inspirations.

Though we feel impelled to run—run—run, the Spirit moves slowly and quietly and we end up further and further away from our only source of peace and contentment. As we insist on moving faster and faster, His pace seems slower and slower to our whirling minds.

Our souls become like a bucket with a little water in the bottom being spun around at great speed. There is no opportunity to fill the bucket. The effort to keep that small amount of water in its place necessitates a faster and faster motion.

We have not lost God or religion—we only possess such a small amount of both that in a hurried society of survival of the fittest we cannot stop long enough to see what we possess. Perhaps we are afraid that if we stop we will be forced to take inventory and face the truth—we possess very little living water.

When we begin to realize there is a vacuum in our lives—a vacuum only God can fill—we find Jesus in a new way. We are aware of our tremendous need of Him in our daily lives. The joy of finding Him is accompanied by a desire for holiness. It is in this desire for holiness that we carry some of our worldly concepts and demands for "instant" results.

We are so accustomed to the rush of modern-day living and so inebriated with the desire for holiness that there seems to be some reason for our becoming holy instantly. The world is in great need, and much of our lives have been wasted in dissipation, so the logical conclusion is that our holiness must be not only different from the past but also accomplished in the fastest possible way.

We can repent in a split second, but the changing of our lives and the conquering of human frailties is the job of a lifetime. This is where Patience matures into peaceful serenity.

It is the work of Dryness to bring about these spiritual wonders. Dryness teaches the soul to wait on the Lord and to learn that if it waits with impatience, the Dryness becomes unbearable.

Inner Patience is necessary to persevere in our quest for humility of heart. If we cannot possess our soul in patience we shall find it difficult to endure the time it takes to change, empty ourselves, become generous and detached.

Without Patience, holiness will take on impossible dimensions, and, like the seed sown on a layer of thin soil, our desires will sprout but never grow and take root. It is necessary then that we appreciate the beauty of God's pruning in our spiritual lives. We must wait and grow during our time of Dryness — grow in Patience so we may bear another necessary fruit — Perseverance.

Dryness Helps Us to Persevere

In the Gospels of Matthew and Mark, Jesus tells us that we "will be hated by all men on account of His Name." He then adds a statement that makes it clear that we must persevere in our seeking of God. Isolated acts of goodness are not enough to become holy. He said, "The man who stands firm to the end will be saved" (Matt. 10:22; Mk. 13:13).

The words "to the end" and "will be" indicate a future event. Now all men are saved by the Precious Blood of Jesus, but all men do not accept the call to be a son of God. There are those who reject God totally at the hour of death and refuse

God's forgiveness. This is the sin Jesus mentioned would not be forgiven.

No sin is greater than God's Mercy, and God extends that Mercy to everyone up to his last breath. It is the soul then who rejects God: God never rejects the soul.

Man does not reach that state of total rejection overnight or by the act of one sin. Rejection of God is something gradual and is made up of little acts of lukewarmness, selfishness, nurtured resentments, cherished hatreds, and egotistical pride — the kind of pride that never admits a weakness, never acknowledges a fault, and is never sorry for past sins. A constant diet of these little and big faults leads the soul further and further from a dependence upon God as the Giver of all good things.

To continue rejecting these tendencies we need the virtue of Perseverance. We need that strong determination that makes us forge ahead no matter what obstacles and failures we face.

Dryness of soul makes us strong in Perseverance because we must exercise this virtue if we are to continue in our prayer life. Perseverance places our love, virtues, and good deeds on a "will" level as opposed to the emotional level on which we usually live.

Most of us become lax in our resolutions because we do not feel the enthusiasm of a newborn Christian—one who has just received the Good News. But unless the Gospel message always remains fresh, good, and new to our souls, our Perseverance will be short-lived, our conversion insincere, and our resolutions weak.

We know that it is difficult to continue on a course of action that is not approved of by the world, or to live by an invisible reality that is opposed to the greed and permissiveness of the world.

St. Paul realized how important it was to stand and persevere in our good resolutions. Repeatedly he encourages the Christians to keep doing good and praying much in spite of persecutions. They could not rest on the fact that they had heard the Good News and accepted it.

He tried to give the Hebrews motives for persevering and said, "You and I are not the sort of people who draw back and are lost by it [suffering]; we are the sort who keep faithful until our souls are saved" (Heb. 10:39).

When Paul told the Romans to be careful and to remember their glorious destiny, he reminded them that, "we must hope to be saved since we are not saved yet—it is something we must wait for with patience" (Rom. 8:25).

But lest they become discouraged, he told them that the Spirit would help them in their weakness. It was then that Paul gave a most beautiful description of the value of Dryness in Prayer: "When we cannot choose words in order to pray properly, the Spirit Himself expresses our plea in a way that could never be put into words" (Rom. 8:26).

Paul realized by his past experience with men and the world and a deep realization of his own weaknesses that man had to persevere in praying and in doing good and had to do this to the very end of his life.

Paul assured us that if we keep praying no matter how difficult it is or how dry we feel, "God who knows everything in our hearts knows perfectly well what the Spirit means and the pleas of the saints expressed by the Spirit are according to the mind of God" (Rom. 8:27).

Yes, if we persevere and remember with St. Peter that we must be "calm and vigilant, because the enemy, the devil, is prowling round like a roaring lion looking for someone to eat" (1 Pet. 5:8), and if we recall with Paul that God turns everything to good for those who love Him, then we shall stand firm to the end (Rom. 8:28).

Dryness is a great aid towards the strengthening of our will, determination, and effort towards holiness of life. It is that purifying instrument in the Hand of God that appears cold, dark, and painful but in reality is warm, bright, and healing to our imperfect spirits.

Dryness Prepares Us for Higher Degrees of Prayer

In the lives of the Saints we read of various degrees of prayer, and in each of the saints these types of prayer radiate in different ways. Some were versed in contemplative prayer at the age of seven, and others were converted only at forty-seven. Some were so immersed in God that they were raised to the third heaven like St. Paul (2 Cor. 12:2). There were others, however, who seemed never to have any extraordinary degree of prayer, and yet the fruit they bore manifested a deep interior life with God.

God is glorified in all His Saints, and their variety of spiritualities gives God great glory and praise. He delights in using the weak and sometimes the scum of the earth to show forth His Omnipotence.

His Infinite Mercy extends itself and manifests His Attributes in the lives of His Saints. Each Saint showed forth some attribute of the Father, or a facet of the life of Jesus, or the power of the Holy Spirit.

Though their varieties of Holiness were many, we find some common denominators among them. They all loved much, and to do this they emptied themselves of themselves. They were all humble and they all suffered — more or less according to their mission and witness. And, most of all, they all prayed often and fervently.

It is interesting to observe that all of them suffered from dryness and desolation of spirit as they made progress in their prayer-life. It is also noteworthy to see that this dryness was a kind of "lift" from one degree of prayer to another. It was almost like going into a dark elevator periodically to rise from one floor to another. As these holy men and women were purified of all selfishness and loved God more and more for Himself alone, they went through the dark tunnel of Dryness as a preparation for new heights of prayer.

If we look at some of the various degrees of prayer in the light of the First Commandment we find there are basically four: The Prayer of Strength — the Prayer of the Heart — the Prayer of the Mind — and the Prayer of the Soul.

Though the Holy Spirit breathes where He wills and follows no format, it is nonetheless true that the majority of us seem to follow a particular pattern. This is not so much the Lord's Will as our own lack of cooperation with His Grace that sets us in a way that is often long and tedious. Though it is humbling to realize we are not what we should be, it is consoling to know that God takes our mistakes and vacillating wills and turns them all to our good and His Glory.

Prayer of Strength

The majority of people begin on this level of contact with God. In the Prayer of Strength the sinner repents and accepts God's forgiveness. He makes an effort towards relinquishing his weaknesses, and spends his prayer time petitioning God for the courage and strength to overcome his faults.

He becomes conscious of his need of God, and although he is not convinced of his total need, he does have a conviction that in order to avoid sin he must depend upon God.

On this level the soul seeks the protection of God and petitions Him for His Providential care in every facet of his daily life. He is faithful to morning and evening prayers, attends services on Sunday, and is faithful to the Commandments and the Precepts of the Church. He is a "good" Christian, but somehow God is not a part of his total life. God is always Creator and he, always creature. This man says that God is somewhere "up there," and he lifts his head as he points to the sky.

The relationship between God and the person in the Prayer of Strength is servile rather than childlike. His reverence for the Majesty of God is great, and though he often recites the "Our Father," the name "Father" is not a real term but only a prayer to the Father of Jesus, who is God and Lord.

This soul is on an "acquaintance" relationship with God and has not realized his Divine sonship. The reality of being an adopted son is not strong in the soul at this time. He is too busy with the business of living and rendering fit homage to His Creator to even think of a relationship that is more loving and personal.

The Father, who sees the sincerity of this soul, and desiring a deeper relationship, begins to prune it as Jesus promised. He told us, "every branch that bears fruit He prunes to make it bear more fruit" (Jn. 15:2).

It is now that Dryness begins its work. The Father creates within the soul a vacuum. There is a void that gnaws at the soul day and night. The soul seeks to satisfy itself by more work, pleasure, and friends, but the vacuum only becomes greater, and the void a black hole that brings fear and disillusionment.

It tries to pray and finds that all the vocal prayers which formerly brought so much comfort leave it dry and without help. It becomes desperate and reaches up to God for love and comfort. It is not interested in asking for things; it is seeking God as a child in need — as one who has roamed the world for comfort and found none — as one who realizes that only One Person can fill this void — and that One is God.

The soul looks to the invisible reality as the only fulfillment of its desires. Here again Dryness does its work well, for God does not always give the soul a prompt reply. Sometimes it seems the more the soul reaches out for God, the further God goes away from the soul.

There is a kind of battle between the soul and God. Like Jacob wrestling with the Angel, the soul pleads, petitions, and tenaciously cries out for help. It is the soul's first actual encounter with the All-Holy God although God's Holiness is still hidden. The soul, realizing there is no happiness outside of God, desires to be possessed by this Holy Lord, not because it deserves anything but because it has a great need.

This state of interior struggle may go on for days or years, but one thing is sure — the soul begins to know its God better than ever before. It realizes that God loves it — loved it first when it was a sinner.

Here is where man learns detachment and begins to give up all those possessions that keep him from giving all to his Lord. He is not only repentant for his sins, but he stays away from those people and occasions that lead him into sin. His discernment is greater, and not only does he repent of his sins; he desires to give up even those pleasures that make life easier to live.

Then it is that God begins to manifest Himself in various ways. Peace of mind and joy of heart enter the Temple of this Soul, and many virtues are exercised. The fruits of the Spirit, mentioned in Chapter 5 of Galatians, begin to take root. This state may last for a short or long time, but Dryness has done its work and the soul enters the Prayer of the Heart.

Prayer of the Heart

The period of Dryness has given the soul a sense of yearning for God. It no longer uses Him as a Provider—one who satisfies all its needs. Now, the soul feels in both an emotional and intellectual way the love of God. It is very aware of the need to love God and to manifest that love by bearing the fruits of the Spirit.

The remembrance of past sins brings deep yearnings for greater love. The love this soul now possesses is slowly being purified. Its attitude becomes more positive, and it seeks to tell others of its good fortune.

The soul is surprised to realize suddenly that God is so close and so good. It is a real revelation to understand a truth one has always known and believed but never experienced.

Everything takes on a new dimension. Nature is not only trees, mountains, hills, insects, and animals; it is a manifestation of the Power of God, the Beauty of God, and the Goodness of God. There is in all of God's creation a personal relationship with the soul. It is as if the whole world were created just for itself.

People, too, take on a new look. They are more than fellow travelers; they are brothers who share the same Father. There is an awareness of His Spirit in each soul, and the soul in the Prayer of the Heart reaches out to his neighbor, not to be loved but to love.

Jesus is Someone very personal to those in this state of prayer. In the Prayer of Strength, God was a name used for the Creator; Jesus' Redemption was a past historical event; and the Spirit, who came at Pentecost, guided the Church in a general way—and that summed up the soul's concept of God.

Now—God is Father, Jesus is Savior, and the Holy Spirit is Friend and Sanctifier. Though the soul has much to learn about the Trinity, it now possesses a new concept of God—a loving God, a personal God. The realization that God is his Father and forgives him, Jesus is his Lord and loves him, and the Spirit pours that very love into his heart to make him a son of God, fills the soul with an exuberance never before experienced.

Joy is an experience, too, that makes the most humdrum day a day of glory. Difficult tasks become easy, and the soul is eager to share his Lord with friend, foe, and neighbor.

God's love is a deep reality to the soul, and this thought carries him through many trials with a spirit of detachment.

Though this stage gives the soul a true feeling of love, there are times the feeling is gone, but he is not experiencing dryness of soul—his soul rests in peace, knowing that God's Love sustains him.

The Virtue of Hope begins to blossom and bear fruit, for the promises of Jesus become personal and something to look forward to. The soul possesses enough self-knowledge to keep it from presumption and enough experience of the Mercy of God to keep it from despair.

The soul in this state begins to forget itself and has a sense of mission. He is no longer a pebble on the beach, one of God's millions of creatures; he is a son and destined for the Kingdom.

In this Prayer of the Heart the soul has a deeper knowledge of the Kingdom of God and the Kingdom of Evil. It becomes more aware of temptation and dangerous occasions of sin. It also sees God's work in its life, His Love and Providence guiding small events to a fruitful ending. There is in his life an awareness of the invisible reality as something real and to be lived in, as much as the visible world. Somehow, the two worlds begin to harmonize.

The soul understands what Paul meant when he said, "Ever since God created the world, His Everlasting Power and Deity, however invisible, have been there for the mind to see in the things He has made" (Rom. 1:20). When the soul earnestly seeks God, as it does in this kind of Prayer, it finds Him everywhere and responds with greater love. Everything gives the soul a "lift" because all God's Creation becomes a personal gift from God to the soul. Even the Redemption is personal, and with Paul the soul cries out, "I live in faith; faith in the Son of God who loved me and who sacrificed Himself for my sake" (Gal. 2:20).

There develops a very personal relationship between the soul and God. The Gospel is "Good News" in a personal way, and reading the Word is a delight. The soul begins to be fed with spiritual food, and the love in its depths makes it desire more and more to give a return of love to its Bountiful Lord.

There is an exchange of Love at this stage, with the soul seeking ways to sacrifice itself for the sake of Love. Then, at a time the soul least expects, Dryness covers it again like a mantle. A deep feeling of loss pervades the soul, making it seek God in a new way, making it pray to God in a higher form—the Prayer of the Mind.

Prayer of the Mind

As the soul makes more progress in its spiritual life, the Dryness that is necessary to lift it to other degrees of Prayer becomes more painful. This is true because the more we love someone, the deeper is our grief when they are gone.

In the Prayer of the Heart the soul began to experience God's Presence, but now God seems to the soul to be absent. The soul feels an agony unlike anything it has ever experienced.

It tries to meditate and cannot; it does more exterior works and finds more emptiness. It gives of its possessions, thinking that the less one has of worldly things, the more of God will it possess.

However, nothing it does gives the soul any comfort or consolation. It is then, in the darkness of its inner self, that the soul is free to see a light it has never before seen.

In its previous stages of Prayer, the soul saw clearly that it must stay away from sin and become more humble and detached, but most of this spiritual activity was on the outside of the soul. The blinding light in which it now lives shows the soul its inner self. It sees clearly that it must not only stay away from sin; it must cleanse its Memory of all resentments, regrets, guilt, and weaknesses. It sees the importance of controlling the faculty of Imagination in order to possess that "purity of heart that will enable it to see God." The soul now practices Hope in a higher degree, for it must trust both its past and future to God's Mercy and Providence.

Dryness shows the soul that its Faith is weak. Faith assures the soul that God is always present and cannot absent Himself from it unless it rejects Him. Even then, it is God who pursues the soul and leads it to repentance. The soul is now led to live on a Faith level instead of an emotional level as in times past.

It begins to seek God "in spirit and in truth" (Jn. 4:24). The humility it began to acquire grows by leaps and bounds, for now the soul compares itself with God and not with its neighbor. It no longer sees the splinter in its neighbor's eye, only the beam in its own.

It reaches out to God in pure Faith and often calls to mind the Presence of God within it and around it. Though there is little consolation in this spiritual effort, the soul slowly becomes more and more aware of the Divine Presence. This Presence is an all-embracing awareness that becomes part of the soul's life. The soul is no longer dependent upon the fleeting consolations that come and go. It becomes strong in the truth of His Revelations through that faculty of Understanding by which it reasons and decides.

The faculty of Understanding that previously caused the soul so much doubt is being elevated above itself through the power of Dryness. It now sees God through a Faith vision. It becomes more humble as it realizes its vast limitations in the spiritual realm. It acquires a childlike dependence upon Jesus for help, realizing more and more that Jesus alone is the bridge that keeps the way open between the soul and its Father.

The faculty of the Will is strengthened at this stage in a great degree. In order to keep close to God in this period of Dryness the soul must exercise its Will Power and mortify its desire for consolations. It rises above the human level which desires only satisfaction. The Will is now turned towards doing what does not satisfy the soul; it is moved to go against the world and its own emotions.

The soul's Will is strengthened by the fact that it continues to pray without consolations and to be virtuous without a feeling of accomplishment. It goes against everything that its own human nature dictates, and, by the Grace of the Holy Spirit, it determines to accomplish the Will of God rather than its own.

When the soul first began to feel Dryness it accepted it as something to endure, but now it begins to understand the pruning value of Dryness. Dryness does something for the soul that it cannot do of itself—namely, love God with a pure love.

In this stage then, the soul grows in Hope by trusting, in Faith by believing, and in Love by loving. The soul must press forward in its quest for God and never tire of the hardships of the journey Home. It begins to understand the ways of God and realizes, in a way it never realized before, that the Wisdom of God is not the wisdom of man.

Dryness Leads to Unceasing Prayer

In the depths of the human soul is a yearning for God that will never be satisfied in this life. It is because of this yearning that Jesus has given us the command to "pray without ceasing" (Luke 18:1).

We yearn to be united to God, to live in His company, to speak to Him as a friend speaks to a friend. We desire to think as He thinks and to love as He loves. These desires and yearnings, constantly living side by side with our weak, sinful nature, create contradictions, dilemmas, and anxieties too complex for us to solve.

It is like holiness and corruption living together as an uneven team, both pulling and tugging at our soul in order to sway it to their respective paths.

We spend much time planning a course of action, not unlike those in worldly pursuits. We sit down and devise various means to overcome ourselves, categorize our virtues and faults, read the lives of the Saints, and then determine upon a course of action and a way of life that will transform us into images of Jesus.

All this is good and admirable, but we soon realize that a period of Dryness shatters our plans and guides us on a course we would not choose for ourselves.

Looking at our virtues suddenly seems futile, for Dryness has taught us that we can do nothing by ourselves. Our weaknesses seem multiplied, and the lives of the Saints, so edifying in the past, make us realize that by comparison, we are like ants looking at giants. Our best-laid plans have come to naught, and we gaze at God with a clogged mind and an empty heart.

At this time, only one thing rises above everything else in our lives, and that is a burning thirst for God. It is both sweet and bittersweet because the very thought of God fills us with love, and bitter because the more we love, the more we thirst, and the more we thirst, the more empty we feel. It is a sweet contradiction and a happy dilemma.

This state is sweet yet bitter, peaceful yet confused, happy yet sad, restful yet yearning, tranquil yet painful. It is the state of a pilgrim content with the difficult journey because he anticipates the end in view.

Without realizing it, we begin to pray without ceasing. Thirst for God and emptiness of heart slowly condition the soul to seek God every moment. This seeking puts the soul in a state of prayer that sets no time limits. Because the Dryness within is constant, the effort to alleviate it must be continuous, and it is this persevering effort that prepares the soul for unceasing prayer.

Detachment, humility, a thirst for God, and great determination give the soul that thrust forward so necessary to arrive at a state of prayer that is constant rather than intermittent.

We must realize that only one thing is necessary—a companionship with God that is reverent, filled, deep, and burning with love—a love that is enhanced every moment by the nearness of His Presence, His action in our lives, His Mercy in our souls, His tenderness in our sorrows, His strength in our pain.

Dryness dispels the cobwebs covering our minds and the superfluities that keep us entangled in a maze of nothingness. We are free to roam the limitless realms of His Love, which are ever there to be grasped in a new way.

This seeking, grasping, possessing, and then seemingly losing His Presence, keeps us striving towards Him in a peaceful attitude of Prayer. It is here that we realize the necessity and the possibility of continuous Prayer.

In all the other stages that Dryness thrust us into, we learned forms of Prayer. We called out to God for Mercy, meditated on His Life, gazed at Him in an act of silent love, and said many short prayers that were darts of love to remind Him of our desire to be all His.

These many kinds of prayer become a habit, and, because of the freedom that Dryness brings to our souls, we find ourselves able to use one and then another with great freedom. We are suddenly detached from forms of prayer—free in His Spirit—free to use wordy or wordless prayers, ready to silently gaze or joyously proclaim our love for Him, ready for consolation or desolation, ready for sickness or health, ready to see

Jesus in our neighbor unhampered by his faults, ready to do His Will and prefer Him to all things.

We finally realize that saying prayers is only a means — a necessary means — to continuous prayer. Prayer in itself is a constant companionship with God as Father, Savior, and Lord — an uninterrupted awareness of His Presence — consciously when we think or speak of Him, and unconsciously when we do everything for love of Him.

Unceasing Prayer is to love God so much that when we are not speaking to Him we speak of Him, and when we can do neither, our heart rests in an awareness of His Presence, doing whatever we do for Him.

Jesus told us that not all those who say "Lord, Lord" will enter the Kingdom. We begin to understand what this means, for we realize now that we are praying when we love Him, but we do not necessarily love Him when we are saying prayers.

The intensity of our life of continuous prayer will vary as our Love is deep, our Hope is sure, and our Faith is living. It takes Faith to see Jesus in order to speak to Him; it takes Hope to speak to others of Him; and it takes great Love to desire nothing but Him.

The one thing necessary has become the prayer without ceasing. The soul has shed its complexities and wrapped itself in the simple cloak of Unity with the Trinity in love and peace. It is truly free.

In Praise of Dryness

Dryness ...

> ... makes us seek God for Himself.
>
> ... detaches us from selfishness and selfish desires.
>
> ... makes us aware of our limitations; strengthens our Faith, Hope, and Love.
>
> ... empties our Memories of self-indulgence.
>
> ... empties our Understanding of doubts and our Will of lukewarmness.
>
> ... purifies our soul so we can reach for God.
>
> ... creates a vacuum that only God can fill.
>
> ... exercises us in patience, humility, and compassion.
>
> ... gives us a deep understanding of the difference between God and ourselves.
>
> ... is the transition period between various degrees of Prayer.

... makes us more aware of the beam in our own eye than the splinter in our neighbor's.

... gives us a yearning for God and a renewed Hope in His Kingdom.

... increases our thirst for God.

... empties our soul so the Spirit has freedom to direct us.

... increases our resolutions to do God's Will rather than our own.

... increases our desire for holiness.

... helps us to practice the Beatitudes.

... gives us an appreciation of suffering.

... makes us see the loving Hand of a loving Father guiding our every step.

... and leads us to pray without ceasing.

This is not all that Dryness of Soul accomplishes for us as we rise, fall, and stumble towards living a holy life. Neither are the degrees of prayer mentioned here the only degrees to which Dryness leads. What is written here is written for the purpose of lighting up our path on the dark road which empties us of ourselves.

Our journey Home will be less tedious and more filled with joy when we catch a faint glimpse of the beauty, purpose, and power of Dryness, and how in the Father's Hand this rough tool carves a most beautiful image of Jesus in our souls.

Dryness leads us gently from vocal prayer, where we learn to speak to God; to Meditation, where we think of God; to Contemplation, where our heart merely gazes upon Him with a love too deep for words.

Our minds gradually begin to think like Jesus and be ever at peace in the midst of pain and turmoil. Our souls reach a serenity that is close to that perfect peace of the Blessed, for our Will and His become joined as one Will.

The mystery of pain is solved because our one desire is to imitate Jesus in every facet of His Suffering Life.

The ability to love our neighbor, previously so difficult, now overflows from that burning love of God in our hearts. We begin to experience in the depths of our being a change so sublime and hidden that we know for certain "nothing will ever separate us from the love of Christ" (Rom. 8:35).

Our thoughts are in Heaven, though our service—unselfish and faithful—extends to all men. There is instant forgiveness in our hearts and gentle speech on our lips.

Compassion for sinners is fed by a deep awareness of our own weaknesses and the humility which is truth.

God's Grace gives us all of these qualities because He is Good. Along with other trials and sufferings, the tool of Dryness in the Hands of this Master Craftsman, chisels away those inner failings too hidden for us to see.

Let us go forward, therefore, with great Trust, knowing that when Dryness comes upon us and our hearts yearn for God as our only joy, He is truly Present. Indeed, He is so close that the brightness of His Light darkens our soul as the fire of His Love possesses our being.

"Pray constantly: and for all things give thanks to God, because this is what God expects of you" (1 Thess. 5:18).

"You have shown your Faith in action, worked for Love and persevered through Hope, in our Lord Jesus Christ" (1 Thess. 1:3).

"Be persevering in your prayers and be thankful as you stay awake to pray" (Col. 4:2).

"Do not give up if trials come; and keep on praying" (Rom. 12:12).

"The heartfelt prayer of a good man works very powerfully" (Jas. 5:15).

"Pray not to be put to the test" (Lk. 22:40).

"Everything will soon come to an end, so, to pray better, keep a calm and sober mind" (1 Pet. 4:7).

"Pray for those who persecute you" (Matt. 5:44).

"When you pray, go to your private room and when you have shut your door, pray to your Father in secret" (Matt. 6:6).

"Then He told them a parable about the need to pray continually and never lose heart" (Lk. 18:1).

Spiritual Hangovers

When we think of anyone having a "hangover" our minds immediately picture someone who is paying dearly for overindulging in alcohol. The penalty for this overindulgence is headache, stomachache, and a general feeling of misery. The body has given the individual involved a warning—a bodily experience of an emotional problem. The soul's lack of self-control has so influenced the bodily functions that death is thought imminent.

Any form of overindulgence creates within the body warning signs of destruction. Too much smoking produces lung cancer; lust produces venereal disease; overeating weakens the heart; drinking causes cirrhosis of the liver; drugs bring on mental and emotional illnesses. As serious as these conditions may be, they are visible and apparent. This is a blessing because both the cause and effect can be used by the soul. Overindulgence can be controlled by a virtuous life, and the effect of illness can be cured with medical help. The soul becomes aware of its weaknesses and lack of self-control by the breaking down of bodily functions. Self-preservation and self-love enable the soul to practice the self-control that neither God nor neighbor has succeeded in attaining for it. There is then a kind of "safety valve" for some weaknesses. When our weaknesses affect health and friendship, we are very much aware of their existence.

This is not always true of other weaknesses. Perhaps this is so because we think we are not always dealing with personal faults, weaknesses, or tendencies but rather the various effects people and events have upon us. By blaming our reactions on particular persons or circumstances, we make whatever unchristian attitude we adopt appear justified. It is in this justified state of mind that we nurse and nourish our resentments, anger, hatred, regrets, and guilt. It all seems so right that we never succeed in extricating ourselves from the mire of evil. Our minds, like broken records, repeat, rehearse, rehash, and relive the hurts, the angry moments, and the disappointments. If this attitude continues for days, and days turn into years, we can be sure we are indulging in a bad attitude. The luxury of harboring a resentment has cost us dearly, for we are experiencing a "spiritual hangover." We are allowing something that upset our souls to hang over for months or years and destroy us.

It is self-indulgence that brings on our "spiritual hangovers." A soul that deliberately harbors hurt feelings will soon experience a "hangover." St. Paul told the Galatians that anger, factions, envy, jealousy, bad temper, and quarrels were classified under self-indulgence (see Gal. 5:19-20). Those who find pleasure in these tendencies and continue to nourish them in their souls will live with a perpetual "hangover." However, there are other kinds of "hangovers." These are different from the self-indulgent ones; these are the effect of imperfections, those sudden flare-ups, acts of impatience, and tactless words. After indulging in these faults, a fervent soul looks back, makes an act of repentance and love and goes on as if nothing happened. However, the soul that tends to indulge in self-pity, looks back, repents, but does not drop the incident. Remorse and regret begin to gnaw at the soul. Discouragement and sadness take up residence in this temple of God and although the Spirit has not left the soul because no grievous sin has been committed, the work of the Spirit is slowed down by this "spiritual hangover." The Spirit waits until the soul forgets its feelings and can once more listen to Him.

Jesus knew we needed to rid ourselves of these long term effects. He seemed to be more interested in the effect people and things have upon our souls, than the justice or injustice of situations. This is why He said, "as for human approval, this means nothing to me" (Jn. 5:41). This is why He told us to rejoice when we are persecuted and abused for His sake (Matt. 5:11-12), why we were to fear when the "world thought well of us" (Lk. 6:26).

What is the present situation doing to us rather than for us? Is the neighbor we do not trust, the relative with a difficult personality, the work that is beyond our strength pushing us down or raising us up to greater heights? Do our emotions control us, or do we control them? Is our present moment heaven or hell?

God permits the present moment and He is in that moment, be it ever so difficult. We must be sure that we do not permit that moment to be the feeding ground of long-term anger, resentments, regrets, and guilt. These are "spiritual hangovers" from overindulging in our weaknesses, our lack of love, our pettiness, and our pride. We must see what Jesus told us to do and how to act so we do not become drunk with and suffer incalculable harm from the "spiritual hangovers" of bitterness and resentments. Let us see what Jesus told us to do to avoid overindulging in the present moment and suffering a "spiritual hangover."

"Never let the sun set on your anger or else you will give the devil a foothold" (Eph. 4:26-27). We don't often think of the enemy getting a "foothold" on us for simply being angry, but the Scripture passage does not tell us that the momentary outburst of anger is the "foothold." No, it is in permitting that anger to take up residence in our heart, memory, and mind until and after sundown, that we allow the enemy to establish a foothold. When anger "hangs over" for hours, days, months, and years, we can be sure we have given the enemy a foothold. The reason for this foothold is that we feel our anger is justified and we have every right to express ourselves in an angry fashion. This may or may not be true, but one thing is a reality, the continuous hashing over of the incident, the embellishment of every detail, and the feeling of self-righteousness disrupts the soul and makes it a vessel of hateful resentment. What is the spark that lights this fire in the soul? Are we trying to justify our anger? Do we delight in feeling superior? What makes our souls live and relive the past? What keeps us in a perpetual state of turmoil? Is it not a lack of forgiveness in our hearts — forgiveness of others and ourselves? We pick, dissect, analyze, and scrutinize every of-fense to justify our anger or make the offender a soul beyond redemption. Whether the offense is real or imaginary, the effect of another's actions or our oversensitive disposition, the remedy is the same — forgive — and place the offender, the offended, and the situation in the Heart of Jesus. St. Paul realized the importance of this when he told the Colossians, "Bear with one another; forgive each other as soon as a quarrel begins. The Lord has forgiven you; now you must do the same" (Col. 3:13). We are to see in the occasion the opportunity to imitate God — to manifest mercy and compassion. However, the imitation of God is often far from our minds. We demand restitution, apologies, reparation, and justice done. This is not the worst. We continue to harass our souls by reliving tense situations and projecting other similar occasions in the future. We create in our soul a state of perpetual disturbance. Every other facet of daily life is seen through the haze of this "spiritual hangover." Our vision becomes double, for we see the present moment only in a lopsided fashion with no light to discern God's Will. The slightest demand for sacrifice becomes intolerable in the same way the slightest noise re-verberates in the head of a drunk. The inability to let go of a disappointment, a hurt, an offense, or an insult gnaws at the soul until it becomes disoriented and confused. The bright and shiny "present moment" is pushed aside for the fog of yesterday and the darkness of tomorrow.

Jesus wants us to trust Him to take care of all our yesterdays and tomorrows. He looks for souls who are willing to see the Father in every happening and then give that circumstance to Him to solve, justify, make right, or straighten out. It is not easy but it is peaceful, for we are bearing good fruit. God is bearing fruit within us, and we have witnessed to our neighbor that Jesus dwells in us.

When we react to another's anger with gentleness we have looked upon that person's fault with understanding compassion and not in a judging manner. The one at fault is starving or hungry in some area — hungry for the word and power of God to change him. To be gentle at that moment is to feed Jesus to that soul — it is to manifest Jesus and feed that soul with spiritual food. The power of example changes and produces fruit in others. It gives them a glimpse of the attributes of God — a sample of the good things to come.

"Do not worry about tomorrow: tomorrow will take care of itself. Each day has enough trouble of its own" (Matt. 6:34).

We may not think of worry as a "spiritual hangover" but it is. Worry is the result of a lack of trust in God's care and providence. Some souls are in a state of perpetual worry. They live in a kind of frustration that is never relieved. There is darkness in tomorrow, and the present moment is lived in the shadow of yesterday. Their entire lives are spent between dusk and midnight, for they never see the dawn of new horizons or the bright sun of God's love and providence. This "state" of worry is what Jesus warned us about. The present moment has God within it to give us peace, sorrow that builds up courage, demands that make us virtuous, and joy to take the edge off bad situations. Our trust in God must reach heroic stages if we are to be holy. Heroism is constant fidelity to our state in life. To find Jesus where we are and in what is happening is to strive for holiness. We are to become, through Grace, what Jesus is by nature, a son of God. We are to be faithful because He is always in the midst of everything. He only waits for us to ask so He may give Himself to us. He desires us to do our part, to exercise our talents, to see Him in everything and everyone.

He is not displeased with our plans for tomorrow or our utilizing the mistakes of yesterday to our advantage. However, we deprive ourselves of grace and God of glory when we live in the fear of tomorrow. That blessed awareness of His Presence and the realization of the power of His grace, will let us live for today, without fear of the future or attachment to the past. His love and care of us is deeper than the ocean and greater than the universe. He counts the hairs that fall from our head. He measures the time of our life span. His love for poor sinners forced Him to take upon Himself the humiliation of our human nature. A God who does so much for a sinner will certainly take care of every tomorrow.

"Why are you so agitated, and why are these doubts rising in your hearts?" (Lk. 24:38).

Is there anyone who would not take sides with the Apostles after the Resurrection? They had seen their hopes apparently dashed to the ground. The one they loved and in whose power they believed had suddenly succumbed to weakness. Where were they to go? What were they to do? Yes, they saw Him heal the blind and raise the dead. They saw His power, but how could it be possible for a dead man to raise himself? They heard Him say He would rise, but who understood such a mystery? The horror of the last few days certainly gave them an excuse for agitation, but Jesus did not think so — He asked them "why" this agitation — why question His revelations?

Jesus would not have found fault with their sympathy over His sufferings, their realization of the horror of sin, or their repentance over their failure to support Him in His hour of need. But these sentiments were obviously not theirs. They were angry—angry at the Pharisees, the crowd, themselves, and Jesus. They did not understand why He let it all happen. They doubted His power, His love, and His Divinity. They were full of "spiritual hangovers." They had indulged in cowardice; they found it difficult to accept the spiritual kingdom He preached. They did not pray lest they enter into temptation. The effect of this kind of indulgence was anxiety, agitation, and doubts. The pall of fear fell upon them and the more they tried to shake it off, the worse their tension became. The appearance of Jesus in their midst only added to their confusion, for they thought He was a ghost. The question Jesus asked was such a shock, they could not answer. They were so convinced they had every reason to lament, worry, and grieve.

He had given them enough grace, and they had seen enough proof of His Divinity not to question the way He chose to redeem mankind. He expected them to trust His Wisdom, to see the Father in every circumstance, to love the Father's Will more than themselves, their ideals, and personal gain. He came to do that Will. He told them many times that the accomplishment of that Will would make them part of God's family. Why did they continue to doubt? Perhaps we should ask ourselves that question.

If we believe in His Love, His Redemption, His Resurrection, His Spirit, and His Providence, why do we rebel, question, and doubt? Why do we live in a state of confusion and fear? Why don't we let God take all the debris of our yesterdays, bury them in His Heart, and watch them resurrect to give us joy, merit, peace, and humility? Let us be content with the realization that He brings good out of everything because He loves us. Let us not place yesterday's Cross on top of today's, for Jesus assures us, "Each day has enough trouble of its own" (Matt. 6:34).

Perhaps the greatest cause of all our "spiritual hangovers" is our inability to rise immediately after a fall and our tendency to react to situations rather than respond. We must begin to see the work of the Spirit in our individual lives rather than the instruments He uses to change us! In our moment to moment, day to day living, the Spirit uses, permits, ordains, arranges, and rearranges circumstances, people, work, and every facet of our lives to purify and sanctify us. If we need patience, situations for impatience will present themselves. If we have a temper, He will give many opportunities to be gentle. In everything we can say, "It is the Lord." When we fail, it is He who inspires deep repentance in our souls. We should see His Presence in our repentance, be reconciled with God, and then go on living in that Awesome Love.

By seeing the hand of God working good for our souls in the present moment, we will respond to that moment with love and humility. We will be able to control our reacting emotions and prevent many "spiritual hangovers." When we fall, let us rise immediately, turn the situation to our spiritual good, repent with love, and continue on with confidence in His Mercy and Goodness. Let us remember that if we see the Spirit at work in our souls in the present moment, we will respond with love, but if we see only ourselves we will react with uncontrolled emotions.

Suggested Remedies for Spiritual Hangovers

- Become more aware of the action of the Spirit in the present moment.

- Make a habit of seeing what the Spirit is doing for you in life situations.

- Look at yourself objectively; receive self-knowledge with gratitude. Bless those who cause your faults to manifest themselves. It is really the Spirit showing you areas in your soul not like Jesus.

- After a fall, rise repentant and continue on lovingly.

- Exercise Faith by seeing the Spirit making you holy, Hope by realizing He will bring good out of everything, and Love by responding with a union of Wills — His and yours.

- Try to realize that life and all that happens during that span of time is permitted to transform you into the image of Jesus. Each moment of that time gives each of us the opportunity to change, be transformed, and shine bright. The clarity of the light that radiates from us will be determined by our response to the present moment and our union of Wills. If His Word lives in us and we struggle to persevere in following that Word, His Spirit will sanctify our efforts.

CONSOLATION

His Silent Presence

That Secret Place

Mankind seeks peace, and yet it escapes him as soon as he thinks he possesses it.

We seek God, and here, too, we somehow fall short of the mark we set for ourselves.

We are impatient over our lack of patience, angry because we are not gentle, and proud of our humility.

Our souls are harassed on every side by contradictions, dilemmas, and paradoxes.

Our lives are made up of broken promises and weak resolutions, and yet we struggle on to find a way, a method, a ladder—something that will finally lift us up from our torpor and lukewarmness, and send us on a way of continuous union with God.

Is there such a way? Can a housewife, a baker, a plumber, a doctor, a lawyer, or a student be a contemplative in a busy world? Can people "on the go" pray without ceasing, and find an oasis to go to for refreshment in the heat of the day?

Yes, there must be a way, and it is probably so close and so simple that our complex minds and complicated methods miss it completely.

Perhaps we are so busy with things, and so conscious of ourselves that we hunt for "something" when in reality we need "Someone."

We live in a world where we are called upon to be very much "aware" of everything. We are asked to be aware of people and their needs, of our Nation and its needs, of the world and its needs, and, of course, we are all very much aware of ourselves and our individual needs.

But what about the needs of our souls and their distraught faculties? How do we quiet our Memory and Understanding when they are out of control? Where do we go, and what do we do when our interior world seems to be going in five directions at the same time?

One day Jesus gave His disciples a new standard. They were to love their enemies, pray for persecutors, give to anyone who asked, and be gentle of heart. After giving them these rather difficult commands (Matt. 5:20-48; 6:1-6), He proceeded to tell them to do two things "in secret."

He said, "When you give alms, your left hand must not know what your right is doing; your almsgiving must be in secret, and your Father who sees all that is done in secret will reward you" (Matt. 6:4).

This is not difficult to understand. When we are generous just to be seen by men, we have already received our reward. The Lord is telling us to be generous in imitation of the Father and to please Him, not ourselves. Though our generosity may be observed by others, this must never be the motive of our almsgiving.

The important part of this discourse is what follows. We were asked to give in secret, and now He tells us to *pray* in secret. The reason is the same. We must not pray in order to be seen by men or for the sake of being considered holy. What, exactly, does it mean to pray in secret? His words were, "When you pray, go to your private room and, when you have shut your door, pray to your Father, who is in that *secret place*, and your Father, who sees all that is done in secret, will reward you" (Matt. 6:6, emphasis added). He then proceeded to give us the Our Father, which is a conversation with God, praising Him for His Glory, and petitioning for all we need.

Where is this "private" room or closet? Surely, God is everywhere, and the Psalmist tells us that if we go to the heavens He is there, and if we go to the nether world he is there (Ps. 139:8). Where can we go that is secret—a place where only the Father and our souls abide—alone and unnoticed by anyone?

In every home there is a closet, and if we were to go into that closet and shut the door we would experience two things: darkness and silence—a kind of thunderous silence. We suddenly feel and know we are alone, and yet the silence into which we have put ourselves becomes a companion. We are very conscious of the silence. It is no longer an absence of noise, it is a surrounding Presence.

The silence itself is not God, but it is a condition, an atmosphere into which we become very aware of an invisible reality—the Presence of God. The silence turns aside the veil that hides His Presence from our senses. We notice that our spiritual faculties of Memory and Intellect are quieted. We are so aware of the silence that it calms our soul. It is as if all tension and trials were suddenly lifted, and we are able to breathe freely for a few moments.

If we were to put the light on in the closet, the darkness would be gone, and we would be aware of everything in the closet — clothes, hats, shoes, knickknacks, and other assorted "things," but the Silence would remain — we would still be aware of the Silence.

We have then two ways of becoming aware of the silence in the closet — the first in darkness, and the second in the light.

Let us apply this principle to our souls. When we desire to commune with God to strengthen our souls for combat in the battles of life, we can close our eyes. When we have done that, we have closed the "doors" of our senses. We have for a few moments closed out the world around us. Now, like a closet, it is dark, and if we are quiet and become aware of the silence in our souls, we suddenly realize *He is there*.

Our Will has determined to seek out its Creator, and for a few moments, in the quiet of that place, our Memory and Understanding are stilled and quieted, and we become aware of His Silent Presence. We can speak to Him as a friend speaks to a friend; we can adore Him as a creature does a Creator; we can love Him as a spouse loves a husband; and we can praise Him as the recipients of His beneficent Goodness.

He is truly in this place, either by Essence because His Power sustains us, or by Grace as His Spirit makes us sons of God. By entering into the closet of our souls, we enter into the darkness of His Silent Presence.

If we go into this secret place during the day, even for a few seconds, we will calm our emotions and begin to have a more childlike relationship with God. We will find in Him a Friend who listens, a Father who forgives, a Spouse who loves, and a God who corrects and guides us.

When we begin to form the *habit* of going into this secret place to commune with God, we shall be able to continue being aware of Him when the lights go on. When the lights went on in the closet, we found clothes and assorted knickknacks. Some of these things reminded us of the past, whose memories are both good and bad. Some reminded us of the future and all the things we would like to do.

And so it is with our souls. We may often close its doors (senses and faculties) and commune with God, but the lights must go on. We live with people and play a part in history. The world around us requires our attention, and often demands it, so we must learn how to keep united to Jesus no matter what state in life we find ourselves in. No matter how much the world surrounds us, we cannot permit it to conquer us.

Jesus prayed for His Apostles, when He said, "Holy Father, they belong to the world no more than I belong to the world. I am not asking you to remove them from the world, but to protect them from the evil one. They do not belong to the world any more than I belong to the world" (Jn. 17:14-15).

It is not being *in* the world that distracts us from God, but being *of* the world that separates us from God.

In order to accomplish this seemingly impossible task, Jesus said to His Father, "I pray not only for these, but for those also who, through their words wilt believe in Me. May they all be one, Father, may they be one in Us, as You are in Me and I am in You, so that the world may believe it was You who sent Me" (Jn. 17:20-21).

Yes, we are in the world, as He was in the world, but He never lost sight of His Mission, His Sonship, or His Love for the Father.

We, on the contrary, become very absorbed in the knick-knacks in our closet. The clothes entice us; superfluities make us feel important; sophistication builds up our pride, and we forget why we were created, our mission, our adopted sonship, and God's love for us.

Our lives do not radiate our sonship because our eyes are blinded by the 50-watt bulb in our closet. Our preoccupation with ourselves has prevented us from accomplishing the mission for which He prayed, "With Me in them and You in Me, may they be so completely one that the world will realize that it was You who sent Me, and that I have loved them as much as You loved Me, Father" (Jn. 17:23).

What is Jesus telling us? He is saying that our union with the Trinity in our souls will make us so holy that the world will know that Jesus is the Lord.

Our union with God must be patterned after the way the Father and Son are One in each other. This is how we will become holy and prove Christ's Divinity. A Christian not only believes; he becomes one with his beliefs. His life must be not only good; it must be sanctified.

Christianity must be more than an adherence to a code; it must be a way of life, prayerful, serene, detached, unafraid, and strong.

A Christian must be a living proof that God is alive, not by how much *he* accomplishes, but by how much God accomplishes in him.

Perhaps we can get a mind picture of what we should be if we think of ourselves as a large glass vessel, filled with the sand of our human nature. God desires that we be filled with the clear, transparent water of His Grace, but we must empty our vessel of all the sand—frailties, weakness, and superfluities that keep the sand so hard and packed down.

Sometimes our stubborn wills rebel, and God permits our vessel to tip or fall, and then some of the sand falls out. Immediately, He sets it straight again, and begins to fill it with the water of His Grace.

All during our life we empty our vessel of all those things that are not like God, and as soon as He sees an empty spot, He fills it with Himself.

Our vessels become more and more radiant with the beauty of God's Love and Glory, the more we empty ourselves and permit Him to fill us to overflowing.

Our neighbor can see God in us as in a mirror, and our vessel becomes lighter and more beautiful to behold.

Sometimes it becomes cloudy as the sand and the water seek to take possession, but when the battle is over and the remaining sand has settled, we notice there is an increase of water, and we thank God for the pain, the disturbance, and the suffering that gave us so much Grace. St. Paul reminded us of this when he said, "We are only the earthenware jars that hold this treasure," to make it clear that such an overwhelming power comes from God, and not from us (2 Cor. 4:7).

The object of our prayer-life is to empty ourselves and be filled with the Trinity. The first thing Jesus did when He became Man was to empty Himself. "His state was Divine, yet He did not cling to His equality with God, but emptied Himself to assume the condition of a slave and become as men are; and being as all men are, He was humbler yet" (Phil. 2:6-7).

Our mission in life, then, is to cooperate with God's Grace, and empty ourselves, and be filled with the Trinity.

We are not to seek detachment to be free of responsibility, but to enable us to love both God and man with a pure love.

We are not to withdraw from the world to be alone, but to be with God.

We are to do penance, not because it erases our guilt, but because it wipes away the traces of sin.

We are to empty ourselves, not for the sake of self-control, but to be filled with God — transformed into Jesus.

There is no definite method by which we can become selfless. Each one of us has particular virtues and faults that make the process of becoming like Jesus different. We must look at Jesus, read His Word in Scripture, and ask His Spirit to enlighten our minds and give us that particular way by which we can best attain the goal He has set for us.

There are those whose personalities are complex, and their way of holiness is varied and changing.

There are those who are simple, and their way will be simple and direct.

There are those who will approach God through reason, philosophy, and intellectual probing.

There are those who will live their lives saying their prayers and offering their sufferings to God as reparation for their sins.

These and many other ways have two things in common: a desire to be like Jesus, and a deep awareness of His Silent Presence.

The quest for holiness is difficult indeed without a continual growth in this awareness, and an earnest effort towards being like Jesus in everything we do.

It is this aspect of our spiritual lives that we shall pursue in an effort to find a way to arrive at union with the Trinity.

Closing the Door

Perhaps the secret of all prayer and holiness of life is wrapped in God's plea to listen — to listen to His Silent Presence — that Presence that penetrates our being and keeps us in existence — that Presence that fills our souls with love and serenity — that Presence that makes us strong when we feel weak.

We have forgotten how to pause — we want so much to keep going.

We have forgotten how to be still — we want so much to move on.

We have forgotten how to listen — we want so much to be heard.

No matter where we are or where we go, we can say as Jacob said, "Truly, Yahweh is in this place and I never knew it" (Gen. 28:16).

He is not as far removed from us as we think, for we constantly walk in His Presence, and He lives in the center of our souls through Grace.

We listen to the silence of His Presence in the quiet of the night, in the darkness of our souls, and in the hearts of our neighbors.

We hear the sound of His Voice in the inaudible words that shout to us of His Beauty in the flowers and trees.

His silent Presence cries out to us when we see Him suffer in the lonely and forsaken. His silent Presence asks for compassion in the downtrodden and the injured.

His Presence, ever surrounding us like a cloak, warms our cold souls with quiet silence — comforting and reassuring.

He asks us to pause and understand His Love, for, like His Presence, it, too, is quiet and all consuming.

His silent Presence, like a bandage soaked in oil, heals the wounds of sin.

Our souls, like dry sponges, reach out for the water of Eternal Life, that they may be satiated with His Silent Presence.

We may lose contact with Him, but He never loses contact with us.

If we are to live any kind of Christian life, we must be aware and present to each other, for when the sense of presence is gone, one of us is very lonely.

When friends become unaware of each other, they become strangers, and so it is with God. He stands at the door of our heart and seeks entrance, for He desires to abide there and rule as King.

He wishes to possess us, though He is never possessive. He desires our heart, but only to fill it with love, so that we may, in turn, give more love to others. He desires our thoughts in order to raise them to the heights. He wants our whole being so He may raise it to His Nature.

He wants very much to be at home in the recesses of our souls—a friend who is always there to console, love, and enjoy.

But the noisy world around us, and the distracted world within us, seem to unite in an effort to prevent us from ever arriving at a serene and continuous contact with God. However, we need these sounds and words to communicate, to learn, to teach, to understand, and to love.

Words are like magic, for they can change our moods and life almost instantly. Some words lift us up, and some cast us down. Some words anger us, and others calm us. Some words make us cry, while others make us laugh.

Men have fought wars over words, and some have given their lives for God's Word.

Some words make men lustful, greedy, ambitious, and proud, and other words make men repentant, humble, detached, and pure.

Some of the words that Jesus spoke divided father from son and mother from daughter. Some of the words He spoke made prostitutes into saints and made thieves honest.

His Words forced men to choose between good and evil, but they also gave thirsty men the waters of eternal life. His Words are always effective and Grace-laden to all who listen with an earnest heart.

"Yes, as the rain and snow come down from the heavens, and do not return without watering the earth, making it yield fruit—so the Word that goes from My mouth does not return to Me empty, without carrying out My Will and succeeding in what it was sent to do" (Isa. 55:10-11).

The Words Jesus has spoken have been fruitful for those who listened, but for those who shut their ears, His Words have been ineffectual.

Words are those invisible sounds that mean so much, teach so much, and say so much. We are all afraid of ever being deprived of the ability to form or hear words, for then life would suddenly become a thunderous void, without dialogue—almost like the void over which God leaned and said, "Let there be light" (Gen. 1:3).

Sounds are also a rich part of our daily life. The sound of music gladdens our hearts. The sound of church bells brings a moment of peace, and sometimes tears—when tolling the time of a funeral.

The sound of a factory whistle means men are at work, and sirens tell us there is danger and make us fearful. Horns and congested traffic rattle nerves, and the ticking of a clock tells us how fast time and life pass us by.

Automobiles, planes, and trains take us where we want to go, and the conversations of strangers make us feel lonely.

We are encompassed by words and surrounded with noise, and we cry out from the depths of our souls for silence—not the dead silence as in a void, or the silence that comes from an absence of noise, but the deep silence—the silence that speaks inaudible words and vibrates with quiet sounds.

The silence we need is the kind that brings us face to face with God in an act of faith and love. We need to close our eyes and realize that the darkness we see is not an absence, but a Presence—a Presence hidden in the depths of our souls—a Presence so close that all seems dark.

Sometimes we must be still and let our minds and hearts speak to Him in words of love, praise, reparation, thanksgiving, and petition. And then, there are times when our hearts are full of grief, and we need only to sigh and be alone with His Presence.

Sorrows and illness of every kind weigh us down, and then it is that we must go into our secret place, weary and pained, and enjoy the cool refreshing silence of His Presence.

God is a spirit, and converses with us in a quiet atmosphere, because our minds are not capable of listening to His Voice when they are filled with noise and confusion.

The Prophet Elijah experienced this on Mount Horeb. "There came a mighty wind, so strong it tore the mountains and shattered the rocks before Yahweh. But Yahweh was not in the wind. After the wind came an earthquake ... and after the earthquake a fire, but Yahweh was not in the earthquake ... or the fire. And after the fire there came the sound of a gentle breeze. And when Elijah heard this, he covered his face with his cloak" (1 Kgs. 19:11-13).

No man can see God in this life and live, because His Glory would annihilate our poor, weak, human nature. The Second Person of the Holy Trinity had to divest Himself of His Glory and become one of us in order for us to see God in this life.

Now that He has conquered death and entered into His Glory again, we live in His Spirit, and we must converse with Him "in Spirit and in Truth" (Jn. 4:23). The beauty of His Nature is like the fringe on the edge of His Cloak; the mountains are like tassels scattered here and there as His Presence passed by during creation.

Everything created is a reflection, a shadow left behind, as His Presence walks the earth.

Jesus Himself spent many hours in the quiet of the night and the early-morning dawn, communing with His Father. These are, perhaps, the most refreshing and beneficial hours of the day to listen to the Silent Presence of God in us and around us.

It may be a sacrifice for us to pray at these hours, but the strength of soul derived from even five minutes of such solitude cannot be measured.

We cannot give our total attention to God and the world together. When we pray, we are communing with our God and Father. We are attempting to praise Someone who is beyond our comprehension — Someone who is a spirit and invisible — Someone whose Being measures every breath we take, and gives His blessing on each succeeding one.

Scripture says, "When peaceful silence lay over all, and night had run the half of her swift course, down from the Heavens, from the Royal Throne, leapt your all-powerful Word" (Wis. 18:14-15). God's Eternal Word, who was with Him, in the beginning, and through whom all things come to be, chose the quiet of the night to give His first act of human praise to His Father.

He was born into the world during the quiet of the night, and He shall be born in our hearts in the silence of His Father's Presence within us and around us.

We are not often conscious of that Presence, because we do not listen to It. A blind person soon develops a consciousness of things he cannot see, and a deaf person develops a consciousness of sounds he cannot hear.

These people do not suddenly acquire another sense to substitute for what they have lost. They merely develop what they already possessed. And so it is that a blind man senses the presence of a person in a room though he cannot see, and a deaf man senses a sound he cannot hear.

A blind person's hearing is enhanced to such an extent that he can almost hear a pin drop. A deaf person's sight is so enhanced that he can see beauty that no one else sees.

All these things are accomplished because one who is handicapped utilizes other senses, and finds new vistas to explore, and new abilities to enjoy.

And so it is with His Silent Presence. There are times when we must close the doors of some of our senses and faculties, and concentrate on the one we need to find our hidden, but ever-present God.

There are times when we must exert our sense of hearing, to hear God—and we do this when we make an effort to be conscious of the silence within us and around us. It is in this way that we touch the Essence of God, Who is Present everywhere. Where He is not, there is nothing—and so St. Paul tells us that "in Him, we live and move and have our being" (Acts 17:28).

We do not often think of moving in God, and yet it is true, for the Psalmist says, "If I go to the Heavens, You are there.... If I take the wings of the dawn, if I dwell in the uttermost part of the sea: even there will Thy hand guide me" (Ps. 139:8-10).

He lives in us through Grace, but we also live in Him through His Essence, inasmuch as His Omnipotence keeps us and everything else that is, in existence.

Our very being is upheld by Him, and we need to be conscious of that Silent Power as It sustains us, rebuilds us, remolds us, and desires to transform us into Jesus.

We need to be quiet and let His Presence penetrate our being by giving Him our wills — and total selves.

In the consciousness of the Silence, we must raise our minds to the Trinity living in our souls.

We listen to the Silent Presence of the Father, and say, "Lord Father, beget Jesus in me."

We listen to the Silent Presence of the Eternal Word, and say, "Lord Jesus, bear fruit in me."

We listen to the Silent Presence of the Eternal Spirit, and say, "Lord Spirit, transform me into Jesus."

And then, when we have listened and become more conscious of Their Presence working the wonders of Their Grace, we can listen to that Presence with our hearts, and say,

"Lord Father, I glorify Thy Majesty."

"Lord Jesus, I adore Thy Divinity."

"Lord Spirit, I praise Thy Sovereignty."

Our consciousness of His Presence must not be negative or void. It must be ever moving, reaching, touching, searching, and attaining the Creator of our being, the Redeemer of our souls, and the Love of our lives. We do not negate our faculties to find the Absolute; we use them to become aware of our Father, Savior, and Lover.

We empty ourselves to be filled, not to be vacant. We reach within to touch God in the depths of our being, in the silent darkness of our interior. We divest ourselves of sight by closing our eyes, and seeing Him as Spirit and Lord. We close our ears to sound, that they may be conscious of His Presence in the center of our souls. We speak to Him from the depths of our sinner condition—poor and stripped of ourselves, waiting to be filled with His Silent, Healing Presence.

Like a lone soul on a mountaintop, we heed not the storm below; we have eyes and ears only for the Love of our hearts, as we wait in silence for Him to speak and surround us with His warm, reassuring Presence.

Like the gentle breeze wrapping around us, His Presence begins to penetrate our being, and we know for certain that we stand before His Presence—understood though we do not understand; loved though we feel unloving; in brilliant light though all we see is darkness.

It is like not having anything, and yet possessing all things; not knowing anything, yet being filled with light. God puts us in the cleft of the rock as He did Moses, as He passes before us and fills us with His Presence (Ex. 33:22).

Like Moses' face, our faces are turned towards the darkness of the rock, but only to protect us from His Glory. His Hand is always upon us, and when we leave our private room to face the world once more, we see His reflection in every leaf, flower, tree, and creature that walks the earth.

His Silent Presence has made our vision clearer for having been in darkness, our hearing sharper for having listened to the silence, and our hearts warmer for having been so close to His Spirit.

Turning on the Lights

With a little effort, it soon becomes easy to listen for the Silence of His Presence within us, but these times of rejuvenation are few and far between.

Most of our daily lives are lived with the lights on in our private room, and it is difficult to keep our senses and spiritual faculties in control. If we concentrate on one of them, the others have a heyday, and if we tackle all of them at one time, we become discouraged and distraught.

And yet, our total person must be consecrated to God, no matter what our state in life. We have been commanded by God to love Him with our *whole* heart, mind, soul, and strength—and we shall never be completely happy if we are found wanting in any of these categories.

When we speak of closing the doors of our private room, we speak of our five senses in particular. We are human, and everything must pass through one or more of these five doors in order to enter into the closet of our interior faculties of Memory, Understanding, and Will.

We can acquire a habit of closing these doors during the time that we are alone with God, and, through practice, we can arrive at an unceasing spirit of prayer in the midst of the greatest activity; but, until we arrive at this state of serenity, we must cope with these unruly senses that are capable of leading us to the heights or dashing us to the ground.

We must train them to work for us, and be careful we do not become their slaves. We must acquire a habit of using them to attain the goal we have set for ourselves—and that is union with God. We must accustom ourselves to seeing, hearing, touching, tasting, and running "in the odor of His ointments" (see Songs 1:3).

If we were to go to Italy and see the magnificent works of Michelangelo, we would be struck with awe and wonder. The works we saw would actually be what was once in the mind of a great man and a genius.

Though the works themselves are not the man, they do reflect, in concrete form, the mind of the man.

And so it is with God. Every created thing is a reflection of God. It not only *was* in His Mind, but it *is* in His Mind at this moment. In fact, its existence is dependent upon its remaining in His Mind. Every created thing that our senses behold or experience is a reflection of one of God's wonderful Attributes, and a visible, concrete example of the beautiful Mind of God.

Just as we can get lost in a painting and forget the artist, so our senses can become so involved in their own pleasure that they forget the author of their delight. They do not see the forest for the trees.

We must perseveringly train our senses and faculties to seek the hidden, Silent Presence of God in everything, that they may serve us well in our quest for holiness.

Of all the images and things we look upon, one wonders how much of it we really see.

Sometimes we have the feeling that we are on a fast train, and as we look out of the window, we see everything, and yet we do not see anything. It's all there, and suddenly it's gone, as some other scene quickly takes its place. When we arrive at the end of our journey, we say the trip was enjoyable, but, in reality, we have no idea of the beauty we saw. We did not drink in any of the beauty that gladdens the heart.

We have traveled and we have seen, but we have no memory to recall, no scenes to enjoy, no beauty to admire. Somehow or other, we missed it all, and our bodies are tired for having traveled, and our spirits empty for want of food.

We starve in the midst of plenty, and are spiritually bankrupt in the midst of riches.

We need to slow down and see His Silent Presence around us. We need to take time to observe the beauty of a sunrise and a sunset, in order to drink in the quiet power lighting up the world around us or casting shadows over everything, and spreading a cloak of darkness to tuck in nature at night.

We need to look at the trees in Spring, quietly pushing forth their leaves to give us shade in the noonday sun.

We need to stop and reach down to a violet nestled in the grass like a purple jewel, and see the beauty of God, who gives such color to hidden things. We need to gaze at the horizon, far in the distance, and see the vastness of His Silent Presence, that is so attainable and limitless at the same time.

We need to see Him crying out in our suffering brethren for relief and compassion.

Our eyes must see more than things; they must also see the hidden Power that sustains these things, the reflection of His Beauty, the beneficence of His Providence, the Mercy of His Love, and the Glory of His Majesty.

If, after the storms of life, our eyes see only mud and never see stars, then we shall miss the wonder of living, and the awe in life. We shall have spiritual cataracts, seeing only blurred images of indescribable things.

We shall cry out with Solomon, whose eyes had grown dim of spiritual insight, when he said, "All things are wearisome. No man can say that eyes have not had enough to see, or ears their fill of hearing" (Eccles. 1:8).

The things we see must not distract us from God, for they are only stepping stones on our journey Home, to raise our minds and hearts to Him.

Our greatest difficulty in life, however, is seeing Jesus in our neighbor, but here, too, we must see more than meets the eye.

In some people, we see Jesus bound in chains by sin, and in those He cries for the prayers of our compassionate heart to release Him and convert our brother.

In some people, we see Him crowned with thorns, by intellectual pride, and He needs us to be humble to comfort Him.

In some, we see Him saddened by lukewarmness and indifference, and He needs our love to console Him.

In some, we see Him smiling, but not yet radiant, due to lack of generosity, and an adherence to their own wills, and in these He needs us to be generous.

In others, we see Him transfigured and growing brighter every day, and in these we glorify His Grace and Power.

In every human being, we see the needs of Jesus in their souls, as He calls forth virtue from us to comfort and glorify Him. We see Jesus in our neighbor so we may help that neighbor arrive at that degree of holiness God desires of him.

And when our neighbor's faults reshape us, we must not keep our eyes on the instrument, but only on the Father, who, seeing our fruit, prunes us that we may bear more fruit (Jn. 15:2).

In some people, the Presence of God is so manifest that He literally shouts, "I am here." In others, whose lives, temperaments, faults, and sins close the windows of their souls so we cannot see or hear Him, it is necessary that the Spirit within us slowly pry open the doors that have been closed by disappointment, and the windows sealed by bitterness.

As we give, so we are given, "pressed down and running over" (Lk. 6:38), for we begin to realize that everyone we see is a visible reflection of His invisible Presence, and it is in that Presence that we live.

Perhaps if we were to think of that Presence, or be more conscious of It whenever we converse with our neighbor, it would help us to listen with greater attention. Everyone we meet has some need that we can alleviate, and when we do, we are in reality bringing out Jesus in that person.

Sometimes we see God in animate and inanimate creatures because they make no demands on us, but we must *see* God in those creatures who are made in His Image — reasoning creatures who can make decisions, form opinions, and exercise a powerful will. It is in these creatures that we must see God in a special way — even though it may be difficult.

To see His Silent Presence in our neighbor — no matter who he is or what he does — and to act accordingly, is the most purifying penance, and the most rewarding experience. It gives glory to God, and radiates the life of Jesus on earth.

We should understand that we must ever seek God, and use everything to raise us to Him. We speak of God being in everything, and He is, but we must realize that He transcends everything we see.

A flower reminds us of His Beauty, the smile of a child, His Sweetness, and both are reflections of His Spiritual, Silent Presence. When we cease to seek God in everything, our souls enter a desert, and His Presence seems to disappear. His Presence is written upon everything, and as we read all the words He addresses to us in His creation, our reason begins to understand His existence and awesome Presence.

Our spirit must reach out to His Spirit, as everything we see manifests His Love, His Providence, His Mercy, and His Compassion.

The works of His Hands, so pleasing to behold, must never hold us prisoners, for they are mere reminders, and stepping stones that keep His Silent Presence ever before our minds.

On the days when our eyes see only the things of this world, the days we are so involved, the days that cares and worries hold us tight in their grasp—on those days, our souls feel empty and alone, for we have lost contact with His Spiritual Presence.

His Silent Presence in everything must raise our hearts to His utter Transcendence. Everything in life is like a sign He left behind, a guide, a living message of His Love. It does not say, "I am He"; it only says, "He is here." It does not say, "I am God"; it only says, "God made me." It does not say, "Rest in me"; it only says, "Let me raise you to Him."

Every moment of life must be used to raise ourselves to God, Who is above and beyond all His Creation, and yet stoops to live in our souls through Grace.

All creation is like a dewdrop on the tip of His finger; it glistens for having come from Him, but He flicks it down to us so we may see its beauty and say, "Oh, show me where you come from."

We cannot turn God on and off like a light bulb. He is the light of our lives and the source of our being. Our souls must ever seek His Face and Beauty in nature, His intelligence in man, His Wisdom in our sufferings, His Providence in our daily life, His Omnipotence in the cosmos, His Presence in our souls, and His Essence in all created things.

Nothing should separate us from Him, for our minds and hearts must seek Him every moment of our lives. All of life is an adventure in seeking Him out, and when we find Him, His

Infinity gives us new vistas to explore and a greater capacity to fill.

Each day is new and glorious, for each day opens up to us whole new concepts to try, and explorations to make. Each moment His Silent Presence hides Itself, that we may seek and find Him. Each cross hides His shadow, that we may take up that cross with a purer love.

His Heart rejoices as we go through life seeking Him in every cranny and nook—reaching for His Hand, and touching His garment.

Our eyes and ears must be open and ready to see Him in every life situation. It is possible to see and yet be blind, and to hear and be deaf. When Jesus spoke to the Pharisees one day, He said, "You will listen, and listen again, but not understand; see, and see again, but not perceive. For the heart of this nation has grown coarse, their ears are dull of hearing, and they have shut their eyes, for fear they should see with their eyes, hear with their ears, understand with their heart, and be converted and be healed by Me" (Matt. 13:14-15).

The pleasures of this world can so dull our senses that they no longer seek or see God anywhere. We are afraid that if our senses begin to see and hear God, we will have to give up the multitude of trinkets we have amassed for ourselves. Like children, we cling to the toys that glitter and amuse us, and never grow up to see the invisible reality behind all real things.

When we limit God to the passing things of this world, He soon passes with them, for the Limitless One cannot be limited, the Infinite cannot be finite, the Spiritual cannot be mundane, Omnipotence cannot be powerless, and Love cannot be constrained.

If we find God only in the springtime of life, when the grass is green and the flowers beautiful to behold, what shall we do in the fall when everything that was once so beautiful slowly fades before our eyes? And then, where shall we look when winter comes and the nights are cold and lonely?

A Christian is one who lives in an atmosphere of prayer and communion with God. He does not, and cannot *say* prayers without ceasing, but he does *pray* without ceasing. He makes no distinction between the spring or winter of life, for his soul ever reaches out, seeking, and sometimes straining, to see God every moment.

To some, the desire to be continually united to God in an attitude of prayer is impracticable, impossible, and improbable.

And yet, we admire a doctor who is totally dedicated to his work, a scientist who eats and drinks his desire to discover a remedy for cancer, a social worker on fire for justice, a man whose only goal is to become a millionaire, and a politician who spends all his time, effort, and money in the hope of getting elected to a public office. We can well understand how men can become absorbed in these pursuits, but not in the pursuit of God.

The first thought that crosses our minds at the prospect of always seeking God is that this effort will cause tension, nerves, and other associated disturbances. It is hardly in the realm of common sense to think that the God of Serenity brings tension, and the world of tension brings serenity, or that the God of Love brings selfishness, and the world of "dog eat dog" brings generosity. The tension in our lives does not exist from our seeking God, but from our effort to pursue the things of this world and God together, and from seeking to be filled with God, but not emptied of ourselves.

The First Chapter of Genesis tells us that after God created the world He looked at it and saw that it "was good." If this is so, why the opposition between the world and God?

Are we expected to wage a war on everything and everyone in the world in hopes of rising above to some supernatural state?

The opposition does not come from the world that God created, but from what man has done with that world.

Instead of using it as a constant reminder of Divinity, we use it as a resting place for Humanity.

Instead of rising above the created to the Uncreated, we sink beneath the created and find depravity.

Instead of looking at the beginning of each day as a gift from God, we rebel at the challenge and the sacrifice.

We do not understand why we cannot be totally selfish and full of God at the same time. We look at God as if He deliberately put us in a difficult position to test our stamina, and then, in our arrogance, we say, "It's all Your fault. You made me with weaknesses, and then put me in the path of temptations, in a world of beauty and pleasure."

How pride has deluded us! He made us strong, but we made ourselves weak. He redeemed us by becoming weak Himself, but we want to be strong enough to live without Him. He wants us to set our hearts on the next life, but we want to stay on in this one. He wants us to die that we may live, but we want to live and never die.

He came and suffered so we would see the weaknesses we brought upon ourselves in a new light, but we think suffering in any form is cruel, useless, and sheer nonsense.

Our battle is not with the beautiful world He gave us to live in; it is with ourselves.

The opposition is not from things, but from our *reaction* to things. It is our attitude, our goals, our desires, and our love that we put either in God or ourselves.

The world and everyone in it can lead us to great holiness of life if we *will* it to do so. If not, it will fill us with selfishness and pride. Since the world can be used or misused, then, in itself, it is not opposed to God; it depends on how we use it.

A neighbor's hatred affords us an opportunity to be either hateful or gentle in return. The problem, then, is not in our neighbor, but in our *reaction* to that neighbor.

St. Paul says, "We know that by turning everything to their good, God cooperates with all those who love Him" (Rom. 8:28). We do not often think of God cooperating with us, but our relationship with God is personal, and together we must use everything to help us towards our goal of being perfect sons of a perfect Father.

"Nothing" Paul says, "can come between us and the love of Christ, even if we are troubled or worried, or being persecuted, or lacking food or clothes, or being thwarted, or even attacked" (Rom. 8:35).

This great Apostle had experienced all these hardships, and he realized that his reaction to them depended upon the thing he sought most in life — the Love of Christ.

The core of our problem is in what we *seek*. If all we seek in life is perfect health, then we shall fear ill health, and this fear will occupy our minds constantly.

If all we seek in life is riches, then we shall abhor poverty or privation of any kind. Our thrust will be geared towards the possession of things so we never have to do without. We will fill our lives with fears and frustrations, as we forever seek the things that elude us.

If all we seek in life is glory, then we shall consider any humiliation as an evil and a personal injustice. We seek a soap bubble that perishes as quickly as a breath. We are so frantic for applause and praise that we seek only one thing — at any cost — the approval of men.

If all we seek is success, then the lessons to be learned from failure will be lost forever, as we become bitter with the world and everyone in it.

If all we seek in our neighbor is perfection, then we shall be scandalized and disheartened at his failures.

When we seek only the things of this world, then we are frustrated and disappointed at their temporal nature, shortlived pleasure, and the vacuum they create in our souls.

Our souls cry out to God to deliver us from our lukewarmness and torpidity. We reach for that invisible Hand to hold tight to as we grope in the darkness, forever falling and rising in our efforts to move forward.

Down deep in our innermost hearts, we know that only Jesus can fill us to overflowing, if only we could tear ourselves away from all the unnecessary pursuits that do nothing but weary our souls to death.

We want desperately to break away from ourselves and our selfishness, and belong to Him completely, entirely, and totally—and yet, each day seems more barren than the last, and our efforts without fruit.

It is when we feel so useless and weak that we can take heart, for we know for certain that we *do* seek the Lord, or else we would find joy in this world rather than bitterness.

St. Paul had gone to the depths of his misery when he said, "For I am certain of this: neither death nor life, no angel, no prince, nothing that exists, nothing still to come, not any power, or height or depth, nor any created thing, can come between us and the love of God, made visible in Christ Jesus, our Lord" (Rom. 8:38-39).

He learned to seek God in everything that happened to him. He no longer sought God in good things alone. He saw God's Wisdom in his weaknesses, persecutions, hunger, and even worry. He used every moment and every breath to see Jesus and be Jesus.

We, on the other hand, separate God into parts in our daily lives. We see Him in some things and in some people, but not in everything and everyone. As a result, we think of Him and love Him sometimes, and then put Him aside at other times. Our entire lives can be lived in a kind of "He loves me, He loves me not" attitude.

We are in St. Paul's third heaven one day, and down in the nether world the next. Some days we are positive we finally have found the secret of serenity, and then some unexpected and trivial thing comes along and we fail miserably.

But here, too, at least we *know* we failed; we *know* we have not come up to His expectations; we *know* we still have a long way to go. Yes, we have made progress while our pride was crushed and our feelings tempered; we are learning, painfully and slowly, to depend on Him, the only Source of Holiness and Strength.

We are learning to trust Him because He hovers over us, guiding our path, wiping away our tears, hearing our sighs, and strewing little joys to lighten our burdens.

He is training our rebellious souls to listen to His Silent Presence, as we realize more each day how much we need Him. We run to Him like soldiers after a battle, for refreshment and solace, and we realize that He was at our side all the time. We become so intent on "fighting the good fight" that we lose sight of the ground we have traveled and the gains we have made — made with His strength and His guidance.

This is the time we gather more courage for future battles — a time we take stock of losses, and plan other strategies to conquer the enemy. Then it is we realize that our greatest victories were the times we stayed close, listened hard, and looked deep into His Silent Presence, hidden in every jeweled moment of our lives.

We can see that the other things we did to stay close to Him brought moderate successes, but it was the awareness of His Presence, strong and serene, that raised us above life's petty crosses and gave us strength so carry the big crosses with calm acceptance.

It is a humbling reality to know that we can do nothing without Him, and a hopeful experience to know we can do everything with Him.

His Silent Power

The creation narrative in the Book of Genesis is a beautiful example of His Silent Presence and secret ways.

When man invents or produces anything of any value, volumes are written on the subject. But the Sacred Writer, inspired by the Spirit, who hovered over the waters, simply and quietly states the whole of creation in less than two pages.

Some like to imagine the creation of the universe as some chaotic explosion, and yet, our daily experience of God's continuing creation is to the contrary.

We live in an atomic age, but how often do we think of the tremendous energy and activity in the invisible particles called atoms. Each atom is a miniature solar system, with electrons and protons, revolving more than a thousand million million times per second, and yet—it is all in complete silence. It is not only silent, but invisible.

Every Spring we witness a show of fantastic energy as each blade of grass, each leaf, each flower and vine push their way through earth, reaching for the sun, for color and life—all in silence.

We look at a fertile egg, warmed with a little heat, and in the silence of the shell, without the aid of any human intelligence—feathers, bones, beak, and eyes take form. And then, as if some invisible, quiet power tapped gently on the egg, a crack appears and a small, wet chick emerges out of the darkness into the light, to play its role in its Creator's world—all in silence.

Man prides himself on his inventions and computers that occupy so much space in noisy rooms and offices, and yet, the human mind, with much more than a memory bank, is so silent that no one but God hears it reason and decide on a course of action.

Great generators operate day and night to produce enough electricity to light a few cities, and yet, each morning half the world lights up at the crack of dawn as the sun rises in golden splendor — in beautiful silence.

The rays of the sun, which so gently paint one flower red and another blue, draw up rivers of water to irrigate a bleak desert miles away — in quiet silence.

Man produces furniture, machinery, clothing, and food in noise, pollution, and confusion, but God creates a man in the small, dark, water-filled chamber of a mother's womb, with intricate physical and mental faculties that live and breathe — in powerful, creative silence.

Man invents large, bulky, clicking cameras to capture scenes of beauty. But the human eye, without sound, envelops whole landscapes, which imprint themselves upon the memory to be recalled at will — all in silence.

Man uses noisy televisions and radios, and the written word, to convey news of tragedy and evil — but each man has within him a conscience, which reacts immediately to good and evil — in thunderous silence.

The machines that man invents to accomplish the work he cannot do, are heavy, large, and noisy — but the nerve cells in man's brain, which originate those machines, are less than half an ounce in weight, microscopic in size, and absolutely silent in operation.

Men produce pumps and motors, attached to miles of electrical wires, to keep water moving from one place to another—and yet, the human heart, created from a speck of protoplasm, pumps gallons of blood a day through miles of veins and capillaries, for sometimes ninety years—in silence.

Man produces energy in his other big machines, but he restores his own energy by quiet sleep. It is, then, when his machines are closed down that he can hear the Silent Presence of His God, in the darkness of the night and in the light of dawn. And somehow, he must rediscover that Silent Presence as it is sandwiched between the noises of his new day.

When man initiates any kind of change, he does so with great fanfare and confusion—but Infinite Love initiates and accomplishes the transformation of finite human beings into sons of God, through Grace—in powerful silence.

If we spin anything around, or move a gear to turn a motor, it is done with great effort and noise—but God has the earth and planets spinning, revolving, and moving forward at fantastic speeds—in quiet silence.

When we drop anything of less than a pound in weight, it produces enough noise to awaken one from sleep—and yet, tons of snow and leaves fall and lull us to sleep by their quiet silence.

Men write, and noisy presses print volumes, explaining the Scriptures—and then, one day, God speaks to our souls in a flash of light that opens up to us the most difficult passages—in calm silence.

When men give gifts, they are sure that those gifts are seen and appreciated, but God often bestows favors upon us that we are unaware of, because He does so in unassuming silence.

When men provide for us, they count time and money, and all the effort involved—but God cares for us, guides us, watches over us, protects us, and inspires us—all in loving silence.

Everything our body does entails motion and noise of some kind—but the soul that directs those actions is as silent as the Creator who breathed it forth.

We are creatures of sound and noise, and we find it difficult to communicate with and in silence. But God works silently: His Grace is silent and imperceptible; His sustaining Power is silent; His Providence is silent; His daily miracles of creation are silent; His Mighty Hand, as it guides nations and men, is silent; and His Presence surrounding us, like the air we breathe, is silent.

It follows, then, that since we, as creatures, are noisy, and He, as God, is silent, we must communicate on His level, in His way, in His Light, as intelligent human beings. It is in our soul that we resemble Him, so it must be in the soul that our union with God, as Spirit, is accomplished.

Our lives resemble a search, a hunt for the pearl of great price, and all our thoughts and actions must be geared towards the finding of the treasure we seek.

His Purifying Silence

It is a phenomenon of our human nature that we do not see the things that are so much a part of us.

So it is that as we gaze at a beautiful painting, we are not conscious of the organ by which we see the painting.

When we hear beautiful music, we become so absorbed in the enchanting melody that we are not conscious of the organ by which we hear. And so it is with the other senses. They are so close to us, and so much a part of our nature, that we lose sight of them and think only of the function they perform.

And then, one day when one of those senses is impaired, that particular sense occupies our complete attention. If our hearing is suddenly gone or diminished, all we can think of is hearing, and we find no rest until everything is done to bring back what we have lost.

It is occasions such as this that make us both aware of and grateful to the continuing silent Goodness of God for the gift of our senses. How sad it is that we must first lose something to realize we possess it. How calloused and proud we have become to take His care for granted.

The physical abilities that we possess are so much a part of the whole person, that we forget their individual character—and so it is with His Silent Presence. It is so much a part of our very existence that we are not aware of our possession of It. We think we are a totally independent, self-contained, and self-sustained individual. We lose sight of the reality of our complete dependence upon His Love and Power.

Although it is impossible to lose the Presence of God, which is everywhere—we can and do lose the "sense" of His Presence, and the results are the same as if we lost the use of a physical sense. We suddenly realize that we had something very precious—and now it is gone. Our souls feel lost, our feelings dried up, and our spirit parched for the fountain of living water. We stumble through an invisible maze of confused wandering, searching, grasping, reaching, and groping for the Hand that is not within reach, the Face that is not in sight, and the Voice that is as silent as the emptiness in our souls.

There are many reasons for this state of soul. For some, whose union with God is great, it is the very light in which they move so freely that often blinds them, in order to purify whatever of self remains.

For some, it is a purification of their love, that they may seek God for Himself, know Him as He is—pure Spirit—and love as He loves.

For others, it is a purification of their Hope, that they may put all their trust in Him, understand their own weaknesses, depend upon His strength, and begin to possess Him here as they will in the Kingdom.

For some, it is a purification of their Faith, that they may believe though they do not understand, accept though they have nothing tangible to grasp, and live according to the Word and Revelations of Jesus, because they believe in His Sonship.

And then, for others, it is a call to repentance, rather than a purification—a call to return to their Father's house and regain the place they have lost. It is an emptiness to be filled, rather than a capacity to enlarge, for they have driven away their Lord by sin, and He seeks them out by the purifying sound of His Silent Voice in the depths of their conscience.

Regardless of what category we are in, or think we are in, the sense of loss we call "dryness" is always purifying, always a source of light, a closer bond of union, an opportunity for merit, a sign of Love, an example of Hope, and a manifestation of a deep Faith.

It is truly a gift from God by which we communicate with Him, spirit to Spirit—on a higher plane—living with Him in His world, speaking His language, and listening to His Voice, permitting Him to raise us to Himself, unhampered by physical laws and desires that are below His Nature.

His purifying Silence frees us from the things and possessions of this world, and raises our poor human nature to His level in one giant leap that carries us over many a precipice as we climb the mountain of life.

We rebel over the Lord's pruning hand as He tries to transform us into Himself—and yet, we cry out for union and holiness. We desire the fruit of holiness without the time-consuming process of watering, hoeing, and weeding.

Jesus showed us how to overcome our repugnance to dryness of soul in the Garden of Agony, when He asked if the chalice might not pass (Matt. 26:39)—and later on the Cross, when He felt so forsaken by God and man.

"My God, my God," Jesus cried out, "why have You deserted Me?" This was a cry of spiritual desolation, but not despair (Matt. 27:46).

As in the Garden of Agony, Jesus realized that many would reject Him, despite the shedding of His Precious Blood. He wanted so much to save all, but men's pride would find the Cross a scandal and a stumbling block.

He loved us so much that even though His Godhead was never for a moment separated from His Humanity, He wanted to suffer all the pains that we would endure, and more, in order to give us an example of what to do when the Presence of the Father was as Silent as a tomb.

In some mysterious way, His Divinity enjoyed the vision of the Father, and His Humanity suffered the deepest desolation. And so it is with us. We, too, are never separated from God, for He keeps us in existence—but there are times when that reality is blanked out of our minds, and we feel a loneliness that no words can describe.

We can endure the cross of being separated from possessions, for they can be replaced. We can endure being separated from loved ones, for we shall be reunited either in time or eternity. But when we feel separated from God, then we are truly without comfort, and if it were not for His Hidden Grace, we would be without Hope.

Every other separation is outside of us, but desolation of soul is within us.

In every other separation, we find comfort from our own interior union with God, but in desolation of soul it is as if our spirit deserts our soul and we are held, like Jesus on the Cross, between heaven and hell.

Yes, in our sinner condition, we experience this to be purified, that we may be born again, but Jesus experienced it out of pure love, to show us the way, to console us when the very word "consolation" becomes foreign and strange.

All His life, His Union with the Father brought Him through the jealousy, hypocrisy, and hatred of men, but on the Cross He was as if separated from the sense of that Presence, and He experienced the very depths of human misery.

He reached the heights of Love when He commended His Soul to the Father in perfect confidence. Jesus showed us the real purpose of aridity: the purification of love, the perfect union of our wills with the Will of the Father.

To know that the Father's Wisdom is in every cross, is Faith. To trust that everything that happens to us is for our good, is Hope. But to express our Love for Him in the midst of darkness and aridity, is the purest Love.

We may doubt the usefulness of the cross, and we may wonder why the cross is good for us, but if, in the face of all this, we say, "Father, I love You; I commend to You my spirit," then we have truly loved with a pure love.

There is comfort in Faith, and warmth in Hope, but when we continue to Love when these seem to be gone and there is but a thread to hang on to—then we truly Love; then His purifying Silence has completed Its work. We have risen to a new level of union, we have climbed another mountain, we are more like Him, and a little more empty of ourselves. Once more we can bask in the Light of His Presence, less encumbered with the things of this world and free to roam on the heights where the light is brighter and the air purer.

Purified of some of the imperfections in our souls, we can better see Jesus in our neighbor. We can see the suffering Redeemer in the needs of the world, and because we possess Him, we can reach out in an unselfish gesture of love and concern.

We can think of others rather than ourselves. We can give, though nothing is given in return. We can love, though we experience coldness. We can rejoice in the midst of pain. We can see the Father, as Jesus did, in every circumstance, because we are more aware of Jesus in people — Jesus in suffering, Jesus in want, Jesus in desolation, Jesus in joy, Jesus in distress, and Jesus in pain.

When we begin to empty ourselves, and to listen to the Silent Presence of the Father in creation, then we slowly see Jesus, the Father's perfect image, in the souls of human beings.

Realizing our own misery, through the searing light of aridity, we no longer look for perfection in others, but only the suffering Redeemer in need — a need that only we can alleviate.

At the last day, He will ask us if we saw Him — hungry, thirsty, sick, and in prison — and, having seen *Him*, did we reach out to lift His burden? Were we loving to the unloved, generous to the selfish, humble to the proud, compassionate towards the hard of heart, and merciful towards sinners?

It will come as a complete surprise to many that what we "rendered to the least, we rendered to Him" (Matt. 25:40). In the same way, we will be surprised to find that all creation was a mere shadow of His Presence—a constant reminder, so often forgotten, of the Father's Love, Providence, and Power.

We shall wonder at how close God was to us during our lifetime, and we shall be stunned into awesome silence when we see how much we have done, or neglected to do, to Jesus in our neighbor. We will understand what marvels of Grace were wrought by His Purifying Silence.

Our Loving Guest

Poets and writers have attempted to describe human love, but somehow, they fail to explain it adequately.

Love is a power that produces and accomplishes. Men have died for love, and sacrificed land and possessions for love. Love is that invisible quality of soul that moves the will to manifest kindness and goodness. Love makes strangers friends, and is a bond stronger than death.

We cannot describe it, we cannot see it or hear it, but we know for certain when we have it, and when we lose it.

Men can love good or evil. They can put all their love in themselves or other people. They can love money and possessions, success and glory, recognition and renown. Whatever they love will determine the course they take, and the goals they set for themselves.

Love is that necessary ingredient that man needs to give direction and purpose to his life. Without it, he goes through life like a rudderless boat on a stormy sea, without a compass to guide him. Because the God of Love breathed a soul into our body, love is an integral part of our nature. We seek love even in our mother's womb. A baby reaches up for the warm embrace of its mother, and the reassuring hand of its father. Somehow, it knows the difference between them, for love discerns the various kinds of love, and seeks to increase itself from moment to moment.

Our life would be colorless and lifeless without the love of family and friends—the love that makes us stand tall and unafraid, because it gives us assurance, acceptance, courage, strength, and confidence.

All of this is natural because it is inborn and inherited. Though we cannot describe it, we do *feel* it. We express love by touch and emotions, a light in our eyes, and sweet words on our tongue. It is a spark that we feel and cling to, a light that burns, and an emotion to rest in.

The God of Love created us to be like Himself — love. Man, however, turned that love towards himself through pride, and then he ceased to love — he began to hate, to be selfish, deceitful, and arrogant.

It became increasingly difficult to love as His Creator loved — with a compassionate and universal love. He began to love only those who loved him or rendered him a service. He could not persevere in loving when that love demanded sacrifice, and so he found excuses not to love. It was then that human life was of little value, for without God-like love, life was a mere question of survival of the fittest. Man lost all concepts of real love.

To redeem us from this state of rebellion, the Father, Who is Infinite Love, sent the perfect image of that Love, His Son, to show us how real love thinks and acts. He would manifest the fruit of love in words and deeds. He would give us detailed examples of how Love reacts under every joyful or painful circumstance. He would light our path, direct our steps, and lead us to the well of living water.

Men who lived with Him wrote down His words and deeds, but, knowing how difficult it would be for us to remember everything we read, much less live by it, He told us not to worry for He would send His Spirit, and the Spirit would bring to mind everything He taught us.

Love sent Love to earth, and the Spirit of that Love lives in our hearts to teach, to guide, to correct, to console, to fill, and to transform.

The Holy Spirit, whose Presence is so Silent because it is within, sees our thoughts, hears our sighs, and fulfills our desires. The very Breath of God breathes within us, for we are His Living Temple. He moves our will, but never interferes with its freedom. He corrects our weaknesses with gentle persuasion, and inspires our thoughts with holy desires and zealous works.

He issues forth from the Father and the Son, and touches our souls with a beam of light that enlightens our minds, increases our faith, enlivens our hope, and sets our weak love aflame.

The good thoughts we have are mere whisperings of His gentle voice; our conscience — the prodding of His guidance; our desires for holiness — the sparks of His Love; and the strength of our souls — the Power of His Omnipotence. He fills our souls with goodness, peace, love, joy, kindness, and mercy.

We cannot say, "Jesus is Lord" without Him (1 Cor. 12:3), nor can we embrace the cross with joy unless His Mighty Hand lifts it for us.

He warns us of occasions of sin by a gentle thought of danger. He instills a desire to set goals and work for the Kingdom. He whispers words of love to speak to the Father, and deeds of valor to be accomplished for the Son.

He watches over us as we sleep, and sets our feet on level ground as we begin a new day. As long as we do not evict Him by sin, He lives in our souls to instill a spirit of love we never dreamed possible.

We were created *to* love, but He transforms us *into* love, for He makes us as He is, and we become more and more like Jesus in thought and deed.

When St. Paul told us there were many gifts but the same Spirit, he was telling us that all the good we do, all the talents that manifest the Father's Attributes, all the virtues that imitate Jesus, and all the thoughts that express love and kindness, come from the Holy Spirit in us. These good things come from Him, for, as St. Paul tells us in his Epistle to the Galatians, love, peace, and joy come *from* the Holy Spirit. They are His fruits in us.

Our problem rests in the fact that we attribute these things to ourselves. Our part of sanctification is to give Him freedom to work in us, give Him our will to accomplish in us, and give Him our heart to love with. He, and He alone, can bear the fruit of Jesus in our souls. He, and He alone, can bestow Grace, for only God can give God to men. His very Spirit thinks through our thoughts, and breathes with our breath, because He delights to be with the children of men.

Like any friend who is a guest in our home, He will not force Himself upon us. He comes to us at Baptism, and will remain with His Gifts as long as we desire Him to stay. Only our own will can drive Him away, when we choose ourselves and sin in preference to Him. God and the enemy cannot dwell in the same house at the same time. The noise and confusion of sin and selfishness drowns out His Voice and drives Him away.

Of our Three Silent Guests, the Holy Spirit is the most Silent, because His Work is to change us, sanctify us, and transform us. It is, by its very nature, a hidden work, so as not to interfere with our Will, our personality, our talents, and our desires.

If we are not attuned to His Silent Presence, we will think we make ourselves holy—so hidden, quiet, and gentle is His

Work in our souls. But as we accustom ourselves to listen to His Silent whisperings, we are soon aware of how powerful and loving He is in us.

He it is who tears away the veils of imperfection that hide the Presence of Jesus in our neighbor. His Love, operating in us, reaches out to the needs of our neighbor. His Strength gives us courage to fight the enemy, the world, and ourselves, that we may "put on the Mind of Christ" (see Rom. 13:14; 1 Cor. 2:16).

He it is who teaches us to love with an unselfish love, even unto death. He it is who breathes into our frail bodies a new spirit, a new heart, and a new mind.

When we read Scripture, His Presence puts light where there was once darkness.

When we are in sin, His Voice instills feelings of repentance.

When we find it impossible to love, He sends a spark from His Fire to warm our cold hearts.

When we are not sure which way to turn, He gives us discernment to see the best way, and then gives us courage to follow through.

When we feel tied down by ambition and possessions, He instills a deep realization of the one thing necessary, and the futility of all passing things.

And then, when our souls are in a vacuum, He fills them to overflowing with the sweetness of His Love.

He is always active in our souls, but in such a quiet, gentle, and humble way, that sometimes we hardly know He is there.

Throughout his Epistles, in places too numerous to count, St. Paul tells us how it was the Holy Spirit who guided him, calmed him, encouraged him, prayed in him, corrected him, led him to suffering and glory, dwelt within him, and finally transformed him into Jesus.

The Silent Presence of God's Love, manifested in the Humanity of His Son, and the Indwelling of His Spirit, raises us up to Divine Adoption — sons of God.

As he hovered over the waters and created something out of nothing, so He hovers over us and dwells within us, to exert His Omnipotence once more, and transform souls of finite creatures into Jesus.

And then, lest we stray from Truth, because we are often hard of heart and confused in soul, He forever dwells in the Church, to guide us to Truth free of error, enlighten our consciences, and instruct our minds to see His Revelations and His Will.

He is our Friend in need, our Consolation in suffering, our Solace in affliction, our Light in darkness, our Director in the ways of holiness, and our Source of Grace. He hides Himself that we may be perfectly free to choose — and then manifests Himself that we may have courage to carry on.

The Father's humility astounds us, as we see how hidden and silent He is in all His Creation.

The Son's humility amazes us, as we observe His gentle meekness in dealing with His creatures.

The Spirit's humility confounds us, as we see how unpretentious and hidden is His guidance of our souls.

And then ...

The pride of man embarrasses us as we see our God so humble, hidden, and Silent.

Before Redemption, mankind could only relate to God as Creator and Lord. How wonderful that Jesus revealed there are Three Persons in one God.

Now we can relate to God as Father and Friend, to Jesus as Savior and Spouse, and to the Spirit as Lover and Sanctifier.

Now we are the recipients of the Father's Compassion, the Son's Precious Blood, and the Spirit's Grace.

Now we can glorify the Father above us by becoming like Jesus, through the Power of the Spirit within us.

Now we can *listen* to the Silent Presence of the Father around us, and see the Silent Presence of the Son in our neighbor — because we possess their enlightening Spirit of Love within us.

Living in That Secret Place

The real Christian lives in an atmosphere of prayer. For him, prayer is not a spiritual exercise that he performs on occasion; it is a way of life. There are times he says prayers, but those are the times he asks for the things he needs. Most of his time is spent in preparing himself to live in God as God lives in him.

He uses every occasion to lift his mind and heart to God, and creates for himself a secret place — a place where he and his God dwell alone. His spiritual faculties are ever seeking opportunities to listen to the Silent Presence, to see the Silent Presence, and to possess that Silent Presence.

His soul raises itself up to God like incense, enveloping itself in the cloud of His surrounding Presence.

A Christian does not strain after God as one seeks a lost object; he merely becomes more and more aware of what he already possesses — His Loving Presence.

A Christian is a realist who fears neither suffering, pain, nor persecution, for he endures nothing alone. He does not seek riches or poverty, for he knows that both come from God and both can be used for His Glory and the good of the Kingdom.

A Christian is a young child in the midst of an old world, to witness to the joys of Heaven on earth.

He is free in heart — free to love friends and enemies alike — for his only goal is to be like His Father.

He is free in mind, for he believes with humble acceptance the mysteries of God, and revels in their magnitude and variety.

His Will is free, for his only desire is to unite himself to God. His love demands a union that brings the Infinite and the finite together in an embrace of Love.

A Christian has a sense of his Lord's Presence though he does not often feel it. Though his soul is often sunk in doubt, it is never clouded by those doubts, for he accepts his limitations with quiet humility.

He wonders, as other men wonder, but he has Someone to go to, to solve his problems, quiet his anxieties, discern his way, lighten his burdens, and share his pain.

A Christian has a power because he has a Presence who is always with him. He is happy because he possesses the only source of joy. He is serene because he lives in the Changeless One. He is strong in his weaknesses because he gives room for Infinite Strength to work through him.

A Christian lives and breathes in the Silent Presence of his Lord. He is humble in the success of his work, in imitation of the Father. He is humble in regard to his neighbor, in imitation of Jesus. He is humble in his love, in imitation of the Spirit.

He *listens* to the Silent Majesty of His Father's creative Power in the world.

He sees the Silent, Suffering Redeemer in the hearts of all men.

He *experiences* the Silent Presence of the Holy Spirit in the depths of His own being.

Yes, a Christian is alert to the Silent Presence. It does not matter to him whether he listens, sees, or experiences that

Presence in Faith or ecstatic Love. He seeks one thing—the enveloping Presence of his Lord.

Once he has found that Presence, his whole life is spent in listening, seeing, and being aware of His Silent Presence.

Lord, God and Father, I glorify Your Majestic Presence in all creation. I listen to the Silence of Your Creative Power as it sustains everything in existence. Your Presence envelops me like a closet in whose darkness I experience Your Love.

Lord, God and Savior, I praise Your Silent Presence hidden in the misery, poverty, and suffering of my neighbor. I see You, Lord Jesus, in both joy and sorrow, waiting for my love to quench Your thirst. Let that Silent Presence be to me as a magnet, that I may always render You attention, love, and concern.

Lord, God and Spirit, I adore Your Silent Presence hidden in the depths of my soul. Teach me to close the doors of my senses and faculties, and be more aware of Your burning and all-consuming Love.

Lord Father, Son, and Holy Spirit, envelop my soul in the serenity of Your Silent Presence, that You may radiate through me, unhampered by my weaknesses. Let me listen to You, see You, and experience Your Divine Presence — in one unceasing hymn of Prayer and Praise.

JESUS NEEDS ME

The People He Needed

Every Christian is important—important to God, to the world, and to the Kingdom. Each one of us has a part to play in salvation history—a part we shall never fully understand until eternity.

We are part of the Body of Christ on earth, and we affect that Body by everything we do, and everything we are.

A broken heart fills that Body with a throbbing loneliness. A smile makes it happy. A joy makes it thrill, and a pain makes it cry.

Sin makes it recoil in contortions of rejection, and holiness builds it up to renewed vigor. Grace is its life-giving blood, constantly renewing dead cells and revitalizing healthy members. The Head of the Body is Christ, and to each of us He has given a function to perform, a part to play, and a position to hold.

Each one of us is vital to the proper functioning of the whole body, and though our particular duty is unseen and unheralded, the whole body would suffer without us.

We need Jesus, but He also needs us. It is not because we can add anything to Him that He needs us, for He is Infinite in all His Perfections. He needs us because He wills to do so; He wills that we cooperate with Him for the salvation of the world. Through our neighbor He reaches out and says, "I need you."

"I need your words of comfort in My sorrow, your assurance when I am sick, your hope when I am discouraged, and your love when the world grows cold—for what you do to the least, you do to Me" (see Matt. 25:40).

St. Paul lay on the ground struck with terror when he first heard his Lord say, "Saul, Saul, why do you persecute Me?" (Acts 9:4).

"Who are You, Lord?" Paul answered (Acts 9:5). Yes, he knew that the voice whose power knocked him off his horse was the voice of his God, but the God Paul knew was only one God, Creator of the Universe, Creator and Lord of men, to be obeyed and feared.

Paul was confused. "Lord," he was compelled to say, but who was *this* Lord? And then Paul had his first encounter with God-made-Man—Jesus—Second Person of the Holy Trinity. His whole concept of God was about to be changed. More than changed—he was made to realize that his God lived in his neighbor. He would soon be aware of that Presence when he was baptized by Ananias and the Holy Spirit filled his soul with grace and light.

"I will show him" Jesus told Ananias, "how much he must suffer for my Name. This man is a chosen instrument to bring My Name before pagans" (Acts 9:15-16). Jesus needed Paul to preach His Name and to suffer for that Name.

Paul's mission from Jesus was twofold—to preach and to suffer. One day when his suffering was more than he could endure he cried out three times to be delivered, but Jesus merely confirmed what he had revealed to him at his conversion: "My grace is enough for you: My power is at its best in weakness" (2 Cor. 12:9).

Paul's mission began with suffering, and it ended in suffering. In between these two periods, Paul had moments of ecstasy and moments of discouragement. But both conditions of soul molded Paul into Jesus, and were a yeast in the dough as it raised and revitalized each member of the Body of Christ.

Paul's entire life, lived in the Holy Spirit, was of value to the whole world—not because he was special, but because the Spirit of God dwelt in his soul. Everything he did, every joy he experienced, every pain he endured, was for the benefit of all. Jesus used every precious moment in his life to build up His Church and guide its members by word and example to the Kingdom.

And so it was with Peter. Jesus said to him after the Resurrection, "Feed My lambs; feed My sheep" (Jn. 21:15, 17). Jesus needed Peter and all the Apostles to lay the foundations of a new way of life—a life totally given to God, a life of joy and sacrifice, a life of love for one's neighbor.

Jesus needed their martyrdom to witness to the power of His Name. He gave them power to heal, to reveal His concern for the sick. He gave them power to cast out demons and to share His pity for poor sinners. He gave them power to endure pain and to rejoice, that they might give hope to others.

Jesus needed these men, and every facet of their lives, to help save the world. Jesus redeemed us by His life, suffering, and death. He needed these men, and many others who followed them to teach, to proclaim, to endure, and to rejoice.

Paul said to the Ephesians, "This may be a wicked age, but your lives should redeem it" (Eph. 5:16). We must all, each in his own way, spread the good odor of Christ everywhere, in order to show forth the power of God.

Jesus needed John—needed him to care for His Mother when the time came for Him to return to the Father. "Seeing His Mother and the disciple He loved standing near her, Jesus said to His Mother, 'Woman, this is your son.' Then to the disciple He said, 'This is your mother.' And from that moment the disciple made a place for her in his home" (Jn. 19:26-27).

Christ's humanity needed John's love and companionship at the foot of the Cross, to comfort Him in His hour of need. He needed to see at least one of His Apostles there beneath the Cross, to reassure Him that all was not lost.

He needed the repentance of the thief on the cross to see the first fruits of His Redemption. He needed the loving sorrow of Mary Magdalene to weep over the pain His enemies had inflicted upon Him.

He needed all of His Apostles, and because He loved them He turned their weakness to their good and the good of the world. He turned the doubts of Thomas into assurance for men throughout the centuries who would doubt His Bodily Resurrection. He turned Peter's denial into a sign of His Infinite Forgiveness, and a source of humility for the leader of His Apostles, that once he was converted he would be able to help others.

When the Christians were brought before the courts to be punished because of their faith, Jesus needed their confidence in His Providence, for as they spoke in their defense it was the "Spirit of the Father" who spoke through them (Matt. 10:20).

Jesus needed Mary, from whose Immaculate Body He took His Humanity. He needed the strong and gentle Joseph to protect Him and His Mother during their earthly sojourn.

He needed the Angels to feed His weak Body and weary Soul after His fast and temptation in the desert.

Yes, Jesus needed them all because Love reaches out for companionship, not in order to receive but to give—not to add anything to Himself, but because He wants us to experience the Joy of being of service, and of being united to a loving, kind, and good God.

Jesus Needs My Service

It is rather easy to understand the need Jesus had for men like Peter and Paul and all the other Apostles and disciples, but we seem to stop short when we think of His need for each one of us.

God created each one of us with a definite purpose in His Infinite Mind. Though He always possesses a panoramic view of our entire lives, this knowledge does not prevent Him from seeking our wills and hearts. We may defeat His purpose by sin, but He still pursues us, bestowing grace upon grace to set us aright.

The very fact that we cannot directly render Him mercy or kindness, enables Him to accept what we do to our neighbor as done to Him. So it is that God needs each one of us to render Him praise and thanksgiving for all the benefits He has rendered to us. Since imitation is the best form of praise, the Father needs to see us compassionate and merciful as He is; the Son needs to see us humble and gentle as He is; and the Holy Spirit needs to see us as loving as He is—all because They are Infinitely Good.

When our neighbor needs us, it is because we have something to give him that he does not already possess. The thing we have to give may not be tangible, but we can fulfill a need nonetheless.

With God it is different. Everything we have in body, soul, talents, and possessions is a gift from Him. What we do give Him in these areas is no gift at all, for we already belong to Him.

It then becomes necessary for us to render to our neighbor those things we cannot render to God, and in the same manner as God gives His gifts to us. We must render them gratuitously, unselfishly, not because our neighbor deserves our benefits, but solely because we want to imitate the Father.

Whether the service we render is tangible, like food and clothing, or intangible, like love, prayer, compassion, and patience, we need to do to our neighbor the services we cannot render to God. That is why Jesus will say on the last day, "I tell you solemnly, in so far as you did this to one of the least of these brothers of Mine, you did it to Me" (Matt. 25:40).

Jesus calls us "brothers," meaning that His Redemption has merited for us the tremendous, undreamed-of privilege of being raised to the dignity of sons of God. We belong to God's family—we share in the very life of the Trinity.

We are to live in Him as He lives in us, and since God dwells in every human being, either by essence or grace, we touch God every time we render our neighbor a service. Our actions influence the whole Body of Christ, for Christ, as God, cannot be separated into parts.

He is forever One, Simple, and Everywhere—and we cannot move right or left without encountering Him in one of His many disguises. This is the problem in our lives: we cannot accept His disguises. We rebel at the sight of depravity, but how much more does He recoil. Yet, His loving Heart reaches out to sinners—sinners who live in darkness and think it is light.

We are selfish in our acceptance of our neighbor, because we do not understand our encounter with God in them. Our neighbor's very weaknesses and frailties are the disguise behind which Jesus lives. He desires to be released—released so He may reign supreme in that soul.

So often, in our complacent attitude, we decide just who and what is worthy of our service. That is why so many will be surprised on the last day when Jesus tells them that what they did to the *least*—the least of His children—they did to Him.

We can see Him in some people, and to those it is easy to render a service, but the least—the ones who are demanding, difficult, hard, and bitter—what of these? Are these not the least?

If a lawyer takes only the cases of the rich, what of the least?

If a doctor has time for the wealthy but not for the poor, what of the least?

If a father has time for his own family only, but has no care for anyone else, what of the least?

If a man has only friends that are successful, and refuses to accept those who have failed, what of the least?

If we love only those who love us, how shall we render a service to the least?

A Christian does not separate people or things into categories. He has one desire, and that is to be of service, find His God, and be united to that God.

The needs manifested by our neighbor are just so many opportunities to render a service to God Himself, and in so doing we affect each member of the Body of Christ.

If a man who is stranded in the desert and dying of thirst suddenly finds a small pond of water, each tiny sip he drinks, no matter how small, rebuilds his entire body. In the same way, each one of us affects the entire Body, and so—every act of kindness, every act of love, every act of virtue, runs through the entire Body like life-giving blood.

Though each one of us performs the same act of virtue, yet each act affects the Body differently, because of our different functions and missions.

When a minister of God preaches the Word of God, it carries a special food for us, because his function is to be the voice of the Body. Those who listen are like the mind of the Body, absorbing the Word, and receiving it in order to feed the Body with the Bread of Life. And then, each member leaves the Church to go out and manifest his faith by the performance of the many services of love that other members need. All of this builds up the heart of the Body — throbbing with love for all the members. In this fashion does the Body of Christ grow strong, as each member performs his service in perfect union with the Head, Christ, and in perfect harmony with every other member.

We are members of one another, and each one of us is vital and important for the proper functioning of the Body of Christ on earth. Without our separate, individual service, no matter how small, the entire Body will suffer.

It remains for us to see how different people, in different states of life, and in various circumstances, all build the Body of Christ into a Masterpiece of the work of the Spirit among us.

Jesus Needs My Weakness to Show His Power

Pain is a mystery, especially after Redemption. Before Redemption, we had poverty, sickness, famine, and suffering. And yet, after Redemption, we are still plagued with these miseries.

This was a problem for the crowds during the life of Christ. When He cured the sick and fed the multitudes, they considered Him a Redeemer, a Messiah, a Deliverer. They thought that surely when God's Son appeared He would reinstate man to his original innocence, in which God had provided everything. Surely if God sent His Son, He would eradicate poverty, sickness, and suffering forever.

But one day, after Jesus had fed five thousand men with a few fish and loaves, they followed Him to the other side of the lake *en masse*. Jesus looked at them with sad eyes, and said, "You are not looking for me because you have seen the signs, but because you had all the bread you wanted to eat" (Jn. 6:26).

Was not feeding a crowd of people a sign? Yes, but it was not because of the sign that they followed Him; it was only to be fed, to be taken care of, to do away with poverty and the need to work. Yes, their kind of God would take care of His children without any effort on their part.

But this was not the reason He came. He did not come to do away with suffering. He came to suffer Himself and thereby give us a sign of His Infinite Love. He bore witness to the Father's Love for us by coming down and *sharing* our lot, and not by doing away with our portion of pain.

"Anyone who does not carry his cross and come after Me cannot be My disciple" (Lk. 14:27). Strong language for a Savior, a Redeemer, One who was to deliver us from evil!

The Cross was a scandal then, and it is a scandal today. We must, however, understand that it is not so much a scandal as a mystery — a mystery that we shall never fathom in this life. We do not understand unselfish love — love that wants nothing more than to be like the Beloved — love that seeks for a union of mind, heart, and will — love that says, "Do not fear. I, too, have had pain, persecution, suffering, poverty, and hunger. Look, I show you how to endure. I show you how to pray, how to forgive, how to love, how to be at peace, how to unite your will to the Father's, no matter how difficult."

Would we have loved Him had He come as King in Majestic Robes, accompanied by Angels? Would He have witnessed to the Father's love for us by being strong, popular, and loved by all the leaders? Would we ever have looked up to Him, yearning to be like Him, if there was nothing about Him on our level?

He emptied Himself that we might be filled—filled, not for our sakes alone, but for the sake of our neighbor. He showed us how to accept indifference—during His Infancy. He showed us how to accept loneliness—during His Hidden Life. He showed us how to accept success—by His attitude to the crowds proclaiming Him King. He showed us how to accomplish God's Will, in the Agony in the Garden. He showed us how to accept pain, insults, and death—on the Cross.

This was a sign of His love for His Father and for us, and this, too, is our witness to the world. "Rejoice when men persecute you," He said (Matt. 5:11-12). Over and over again, He told us not to be afraid, for He had conquered the world (see Jn. 16:33). He conquered—not by changing *it*, but by changing the men who lived in it.

He gave up everything for us, and He wants His disciples to do the same. Privation was part of His witness—it must be part of ours. "And He instructed His followers to take nothing for the journey except a staff—no bread, no haversack, no coppers for their purses. They were to wear sandals, but, He added, 'Do not take a spare tunic'" (Mk. 6:8-9).

As Jesus was a witness of the Father's love, so His followers are to be witnesses of Jesus' love. As He showed His love by privation, suffering, and death, so His followers must be witnesses to the world that Jesus is Lord, Jesus is God, Jesus is Savior.

Our witness is not to be healthy, wealthy, and wise, but to accept whatever Providence sends our way, with joy of heart and peace of mind — in sickness or health, in poverty or riches, in success or failure. Our witness is to be truly free — free in mind, with no resentments to disturb us; free in heart with no attachments to hamper us; free in body, living in self-control; and free in spirit, ever seeking union with God and His Honor and Glory.

Before Redemption, men of God determined their holiness of life by the evidence of God's blessings as manifested by material success, health, friends, and large families. Suffering and poverty were considered as punishments visited upon sinners, and to die on the cross was a visible sign of being cursed (Gal. 3:13).

Jesus became "completely like us so that He could be compassionate and trustworthy.... Because He has Himself been through temptations, He is able to help others who are tempted" (Heb. 2:18). He took upon Himself the suffering that the world considered an evil, and gave it power in the hands of a Christian, to change the world. "Although He was Son, He learnt to obey through suffering.... Suffering is part of your training.... He does it all for our own good, so that we may share His own Holiness" (Heb. 5:8; 12:7, 10).

He has given us the opportunity to keep our eyes on Him so that our faith will lead us to holiness, in order that we in turn may be a beacon light to our neighbors, and by our own patience and joy in suffering may lead them as He leads us.

"It was appropriate that God, for whom everything exists, should make perfect through suffering the Leader who would take them to their salvation. For the *One who sanctifies, and the ones who are sanctified*, are of the *same* stock" (Heb. 2:10-11, emphasis added).

We, as Christians, are one with our Leader, and that is why He has promised us that, as He was misunderstood by the world, we, too, will be misunderstood.

Being misunderstood showed He thought not as man thinks, but as God thinks. His method and way of Redemption was totally contrary to man's idea of Redemption. His way to attain holiness was contrary to man's idea of holiness. He redeemed us in the way the Father decreed, and all those who desire to follow Him must follow the same pattern — must manifest the same unselfish love—must manifest the same courage and detachment, and bear the same witness—a witness, not in words alone, but in example.

Jesus used the evil consequences of original sin by experiencing them in His own Person, and thereby making them powerful tools of merit and witness.

As we needed His witness of love and sacrifice, He needs ours in order to show the world the power that is manifest in weakness.

"These same works of Mine testify that the Father has sent Me" (Jn. 5:36). His "works" were not only His miracles, but His entire life from His Incarnation to His Ascension.

He was "at work" when He was born in a cold cave, fled into Egypt, labored as a carpenter, was tempted in the desert, was alone at prayer in the cool of the night, preached to the multitudes, showed mercy to sinners, was gentle to the arrogant, and suffered on the Cross. Every moment of His life was work, and He spoke often of working while it was "light," and of the "hour" of His Passion (Jn. 2:4; 9:4; 12:27).

His entire life was a labor of love for poor sinners as He radiated the love and compassion of God. He had a deep sense of mission, and His disciples followed His example.

For Peter, Paul, and all the Christians, every moment of their lives had meaning and purpose—not only for themselves, but for the world. He told them, "As the Father sent Me, so am I sending you" (Jn. 20:21). These first Christians did not waste time wondering what to do for God: they knew that every moment of their daily lives passed through the loving hands of the Father, who put upon it His stamp of approval.

Jesus had told them, "In the world you will have trouble, but be brave: I have conquered the world." "The hour is coming when anyone who kills you will think he is doing a holy duty for God." And so it was that when the Apostles were called in before the Sanhedrin, who had them flogged, they *rejoiced* that they were found worthy to suffer for the name of Jesus (Jn. 16:33; Acts 5:41).

These men did not separate events or people into categories, some of which were important and some unimportant. Every event, pleasant or unpleasant, every Christian, famous or unknown, was a necessary and important part of the Body of Christ and salvation history.

Each Christian had a sense of mission, though that mission be known to God alone. Each had a sense of belonging, a sense of being needed and necessary, no matter how unknown or insignificant he was in the eyes of the world. Each was a part of the Mystery of Christ's Body on earth, and that privilege made everything he said and did in union with that Body, precious in the sight of God and beneficial to the world.

One day, Paul said to the Colossians in an exultant tone of voice, "It makes me happy to suffer for you, as I am suffering now, and in my body to do what I can to make up all that has still to be undergone by Christ, for the sake of His Body, the Church" (Col. 1:24). When Paul suffered, it was Christ who suffered, and for the good of all the Church — of each member who makes up that living Temple.

The first Christians never lost sight of their vocation to be living, vibrant members of Christ's Body on earth. To belong to Him made them powerful with His Power. To believe in Him filled them with His Spirit. To suffer for His name made them witness to the glory to come. To love one another made them witness that Jesus was Lord. To be filled with joy proved to the world there was a Kingdom beyond.

No Christian ever felt lonely or useless — he was not looking for applause and approval. The realization of bearing within his very soul the Divine Indwelling of Father, Son, and Holy Spirit, made each one a powerful tool for the salvation of the world.

Each Christian was a powerhouse of grace, reaching out and touching a neighbor by example and prayer. He was powerful no matter where he was or what he did, for the power he possessed was not his own, but the Power of Him who dwelt within, and in whom he "lived and moved and had his being" (Acts 17:28).

It was especially when he was weak that he was strong, for then he truly resembled his Master, who was "crucified through weakness, but lives now through the Power of God. So then, we are weak, as He was, but we shall live with Him, through the Power of God, *for your benefit*" (2 Cor. 13:4). Our weakness benefits the whole Body of Christ on earth, because He lives in us, and "God's weakness is stronger than human strength" (1 Cor. 1:25).

This realization of power in weakness, joy in pain, and love without measure gave the first Christians an exhilarating attitude of expectation. They looked forward to the Kingdom, and to the time when they would see the hidden and silent Presence of their God, face to face. They would see how beautifully every joy and tear in their earthly lives aided their Mighty God in the salvation of His People. They would then experience in full what they experienced in part — the freedom, love, and joy of the children of God.

They saw a purpose to everything in life. Paul said to the Corinthians, "Indeed, as the sufferings of Christ overflow to us, so, through Christ does our consolation flow" (2 Cor. 1:5). These men saw Jesus in everything; they saw hidden mysteries behind common, ordinary, humdrum happenings.

Today, when we suffer, all we see is the misery of it all — a purposeless waste of precious time. But Paul and the first Christians saw more, for Paul said, "When we are made to suffer, it is for your consolation and salvation.... A gentle Father comforts us in all our sorrows, so that we can offer others, in their sorrows, the consolation we have received from God" (2 Cor. 1:4, 6).

These men lived in an endless circle of combined effort in Christ to save the world, help each other, render a service, attain a common goal, and live together in the Kingdom of Heaven. Jesus in them and they in Jesus, were never wanting in purpose, in goal, in love, in desire, and in fulfillment. "We are Christ's incense to God," Paul told these men, and every moment of their lives rose up to God like a pleasing fragrance, joining them to Christ — blending, harmonizing, and uniting them with the Head of the Body, and offering to the Father a continuous sacrifice of praise (2 Cor. 2:14).

Every Christian was and is "a letter from Christ" to the world, "written, not with ink, but with the Spirit of the living God," written, "not on stone tablets, but in their living hearts" (2 Cor. 3:3).

Every retarded, deformed, crippled, handicapped, or senile person, who has been baptized, is a powerhouse for good in a wicked world, by reason of the grace of God that dwells in his soul. He need not understand or be able to explain that grace. It is enough that he possesses it. His presence in the world makes that world, and everyone in it, better for his having been born, even though he himself may have little communication with that world. He is a vessel that carries the light of the living God in a dark world.

The aged and lonely, whose lives are considered useless because they cannot produce at their fullest capacity, are veritable dynamos of spiritual energy when their souls possess the Presence of the Trinity through grace; their minds possess the wisdom that comes from experience; their spirits possess the serenity of those who have fought the good fight and wait with joy for the call of the Master.

There are no barriers for Christians who work together with their Leader, Christ, for the good of all. Each one is an important and a precious part of the whole. Rich and poor, sick and healthy, young and old, illiterate and genius—all work together in the Divine Presence which dwells in each one as in a living Temple.

Jesus needs them all, as some build by teaching, some repair by repentance, some make reparation by suffering, some enhance by joy, some guide by ministering, some heal by loving care, some provide by working and some enliven by loving. Whatever is their portion, the Christian is a light, a beacon, and an integral part of the Mystical Body of Christ.

Jesus Needs My Repentance to Forgive

John the Baptist stood on the bank of the Jordan and said, "I baptize you in water for repentance, but the One who follows me is more powerful than I am, and I am not fit to carry His sandals; He will baptize you with the Holy Spirit and fire" (Matt. 3:11).

Everything John did was a prelude to the coming of Jesus and the Spirit—even his *kind* of repentance. The repentance of John opened the minds and consciences of men. It gave a deep awareness and sorrow for the depth of their sins. But that kind of repentance was merely the beginning of the kind born of the Spirit.

John's repentance prepared the soil of men's hearts to receive the life-giving Spirit and His Grace. It did not, and could not, make men sons of God—only creatures deeply sorry for offending their Creator. The relationship was one of fear and, as such, lacked the power to change the heart.

John's repentance was an intellectual awareness of wrongdoing, and it prepared the heart to receive the Divine Healer in order to begin to change that heart from a heart of stone into a heart on fire with God's own love.

John told the people their sins. He brought out those sins in public and cast fear into every heart. He made them take inventory of their lives, made them take stock of their motives, made them realize that there comes a time in life when a man must look at his soul as it stands before God, and humbly strike his breast in recognition of his offenses.

This was John's real mission—to prepare the way of the Lord—to make men stop and look up to their God in a sincere acknowledgment of their need for a Savior. Unless these people understood their need for a Savior, unless they looked forward with great expectation, they ran the risk of missing

Him completely. But John fulfilled his mission well, and everyone flocked to the Jordan, ready and anxious to be baptized in the water of repentance — the first cleansing in preparation for the fire of the Holy Spirit.

Today, many people never pass that stage of repentance. They exhibit sorrow, contrition, need, and fear, but their repentance never rises to the level of loving change. And this is the difference between the repentance inspired by John and the repentance inspired by Jesus.

Jesus made all those who heard His Voice deeply aware that they had offended a Father who loved them so much He sent His own Son as Savior. He spoke of Heaven and the Kingdom, of loving them more than a mother loves a child, of forgiveness and mercy, of compassion and kindness. He spoke of suffering as though it were a rare privilege, of God's Will being food for the soul, of confidence in the Father's Providence, and the promise of the Spirit who would come and dwell in their hearts.

Everything Jesus did and said inspired broken hearts, repentant hearts, lonely hearts, fearful hearts, doubtful hearts, and cold hearts, to a total dedication and complete change. Their desire was to change so that they might become like Him, to think like Him, to love like Him, and to act like Him. Their repentance was born of love, and love made that repentance deep and lasting, because it bore the fruit of a new life.

Jesus never called the woman taken in adultery a sinner, but His compassion made the very marrow of her bones quiver with repentance because He looked at her with such understanding love. Yes, she would sin no more, because that sin deeply hurt a loving God. He was hurt, because when she defiled her body she defiled His Image in her soul. She blurred that Image until it was barely visible and thus decreased her chance to enter the Kingdom and be with Him for all eternity.

This poor woman must have sensed His infinite and totally unselfish love, and in that light she saw herself and her soul. Yes, she would never again defile that Temple — she would receive His Merciful love — she would repent out of love — and she would change her life.

We see this loving and powerful repentance in the life of Mary Magdalene, in Peter, in Matthew, in Zacchaeus, and in the thief on the cross. Each one had much to be sorry for, and the loving Mercy extended to them by God's Son, melted their hearts, changed their attitudes, gave them hope, and inspired a joyful humility. This humility made them admit their failures with a deep awareness of their need for a Savior, and the total forgiveness of that Savior. Their hearts, humbled by sin, became exuberant with joy over the realization that they were loved so very much by their God.

St. John tells us in his first Epistle, "God's love for us was revealed when God sent into the world His only Son, so that we could have life through Him; this is the love I mean: *not our love for God, but God's love for us*" (1 Jn. 4:10, emphasis added).

This reality brought forth from sinners not only a sorrowful repentance, but also the Will to make a complete change in their lives. When temptation buffeted their pure souls, God's love gave them the courage to carry on despite the struggle. They found their God and nothing would ever separate them again. This is the repentance born of the Spirit, and made beautiful before the Throne of God by the fire of love.

The fear inspired by the Baptist's message of repentance that made them aware of sin and their need of a Savior was replaced by love. St. John was to say, "In love there can be no fear, but fear is driven out by perfect love: because to fear is to expect punishment, and anyone who is afraid is still imperfect in love. We are to love, then, because He loved us first" (1 Jn. 4:18-19).

The knowledge of God's love for poor sinners "filled in every valley, laid low every mountain, straightened winding ways, and made rough roads smooth" in their lives (Lk. 3:5). The Baptist knew that his kind of repentance was only the beginning, for he told the people, "If you are repentant, produce the appropriate fruits.... Any tree which fails to produce good fruit will be cut down and thrown on the fire" (Lk. 3:8-9).

The repentant Christian, whose repentance is fed by humility, grows through love and bears the fruit of self-control, giving witness to the whole world of God's love for us. He gives courage to sinners and hope to the despairing. He cries out in joy, "Look, take courage; God loves *you*. He sent His own Son to save you. He wants to make you a son, fill you with grace, embrace you in love, and let all of Heaven rejoice that you desire Him above all things."

In the Temple the Pharisee concentrated on his love for God and thought he had no need for repentance (Lk. 18:9-14). The sinner, aware of his weakness and crying out for mercy, became aware of God's love for him. The Pharisee had illusions of grandeur, never acknowledging his sinner condition, never opening his soul to receive the waters of forgiveness and the rebirth of a new life. He grew in pride. His heart hardened, and his eyes were blinded to the Presence of the Messiah.

Today, many who count their good deeds and determine each day the measure of *their* love for God, run the risk of hardening their hearts and never witnessing to the Power of Christian repentance.

Jesus needs our loving repentance in order to flood our souls with grace and the new life. You cannot put water into a sealed jar, and neither can God put grace into a proud, hardened heart.

The Pharisee ended up with no need for repentance, for he was perfect in his own eyes. The thought of any failure or weakness on his part was repugnant to him. He sought the perfection that came from the Law and himself. He wanted a perfection he could see and arrive at on his own. He wanted to *feel* holy and good, and anything to the contrary made him uneasy and discouraged. So he would do the things he thought holy people did, and follow the Law so all could see what *he* wanted to see — his perfection.

The poor sinner, who anointed the Lord's feet with expensive ointment, had no idea her actions would be recorded in the Gospels for all men to read. Jesus prophesied it would be so, for He wanted all of us to know the power of repentant love (Matt. 26:6-13). Preachers may speak about repentance in glowing terms, but the sinner who lovingly repents and changes his life speaks a sermon without words, manifests the Mercy of God, and portrays the peace that surpasses understanding (Phil. 4:7).

Jesus told Peter that once he was converted, that is, repentantly aware of his weakness, he would confirm his brethren (Lk. 22:32). This does not mean that we must sin to understand the sinner, but it does mean that when and if we have had the misfortune to sin, we can be more compassionate towards others. We can have empathy towards our brother and manifest the humility so necessary to help convert other men.

As our sins can destroy, so our repentance and change of life can rebuild. In rebuilding we give hope to the world and to all those who struggle with the discouragement that comes from resolutions never kept, promises never fulfilled, and goals never attained.

Our sincere repentance is necessary in the world today. Jesus needs it to attract others to repentance. Paul was very conscious of this particular mission for each Christian, when he said to the Corinthians, "It was God who reconciled us to Himself through Christ, and gave *us the work* of handing on this reconciliation — we are ambassadors for Christ; *it is as though God were appealing through us,* and the appeal we make in Christ's name is: be reconciled to God" (2 Cor. 5:18, 20).

God has given each one of us the mission of telling the world, by word and example, that God has reconciled us with Himself through the loving Heart of Jesus. Through our personal repentance and change of life, and the example of "a new creation," God shows forth to other men, His Infinite Mercy and Love (2 Cor. 5:17). He needs our repentance to encourage sinners to repent and assure them of God's Mercy and Love.

Jesus Needs My Love

At the end of Christ's priestly prayer during the Last Supper discourse, He gave us an idea of how to please Him, and how to show the world His love.

"With Me in them and You in Me, may they be so completely one that the world will realize that it was You who sent Me, and that I have loved them as much as You loved me" (Jn. 17:23-24). It is truly a marvelous assignment that the Lord has given to each Christian. With Jesus dwelling in our souls through Baptism, we are to prove to the world by our love for

Jesus that the Father sent Him, and that Jesus loves us as much as the Father loves Him.

His desire that we be "so completely one with Him" has a ring of urgency, a burning desire that we love Him as much as He loves us. When two people love each other, that very love proves to everyone that they belong together. Love proves that certain individuals in our lives are friends, and a lack of it proves that other people are merely acquaintances, or even enemies.

Our love for people proves that we are emotionally well balanced, and a lack of love proves that something has warped our personality and made us hard and bitter.

Love proves that we have a healthy interest in our neighbor, and a lack of love proves a cold indifference that can be cruel.

Love proves its power by melting icy hearts, giving assurance, changing personalities, instilling joy, and promoting a feeling of well-being that nothing else can accomplish.

Love proves that we care — care enough to sacrifice for the good of another. Love needs to prove itself; it strains to give proof of its intensity, and is ingenious in its way of providing that proof.

Many of us have lost the "proving" quality of our love for God, and have forgotten the power that proof exerts on other people. We have lost sight of that powerful passage of Scripture, tucked away at the end of the Last Supper discourse, that tells us our union with God will prove Jesus is Lord, and that He truly loves each one of us, personally and individually.

We cannot and must not love just for the sake of proving something. Love is so delicate and fragile in its strength that as soon as we begin to use it to prove something, we have lost it.

The proof that comes from true love is hidden and unnoticed by the one who possesses it. The reason for this is that the person who loves God deeply and continues to love Him is so busy loving, he is not aware of his witness—the witness is the *fruit* of a deep love, not the cause of that love.

So it was with the first Christians. The pagans were attracted to Jesus, not so much by preaching, as by the love each of the brethren manifested towards the other. They proved His Divinity by that love. Only the grace that comes from God Himself can make people love each other deeply, share each other's sorrows, rejoice in each other's good fortune, lose possessions, homes, and land with a spirit of detachment and rejoice when they are considered fools.

"The whole group of believers was united, heart and soul; no one claimed for his own use anything that he had, as everything they owned was held in common" (Acts 4:32).

Only God could accomplish such wonders in the hearts of men who were once selfish, proud, and greedy individuals. A real change of life, with a deep, loving concern for one's neighbor, proved to pagans that Jesus was God's Son.

We live in a world that exhibits only selfish love—love that is maintained by the service rendered. Selfish love is measured by what we gain, rather than what we give, and so it consumes rather than transforms. It is repulsed by everyone when seen in others, and yet, each one of us has it in some degree. It never lifts up or bears witness to goodness. If it proves anything, it proves how human our nature is, and how impossible it is to lift ourselves above ourselves. Selfish love is common to our nature, and only grace from God can lift us above this human frailty. This is so obvious that when we find anyone loving, compassionate, kind, and merciful, we immediately think of God.

The People of God, in the time of Jesus, believed in the one God, and, although they expected a Messiah, they thought in terms of a great man, a deliverer, a Prophet, a man sent by God, a man like David, Isaiah, or Jeremiah. They never dreamed of the Father sending His only Son—God-made-Man. The mystery of the Trinity was not yet revealed, and the thought of two or three Persons in one God was blasphemy to them.

It was necessary then that Jesus prove His Divinity by doing the works of God—miracles of body and soul. The healing of the body was needed so faith would be increased in the people, but the "greatest work" of all was the work of changing hearts and souls—changing them so completely that it was obvious to everyone that God Himself had intervened in their lives. In this way, the followers of Jesus proved to the world that Jesus was truly God. Love and devotion for Jesus changed their lives, and that change also wrought wonders in the lives of others.

Jesus needs our change of life to prove to pagans that He is God's Son and worthy of love and adoration. Jesus changes us into a beautiful image of Himself, through the Power of the Holy Spirit living in our hearts. He is our exemplar and pattern—our Savior and hope, our Mediator with the Father. This reality cannot be stagnant in our lives. As Christians, our love for Jesus must be manifested by more than just works. We must have a deep awareness of God's love for us. This is the Good News. Love cannot be one-sided, and the realization that God loved us first, must be an unending source of joy and hope. This is the joy and hope that must be manifested to our neighbor.

Jesus needs each one of us to preach this revelation — not by words, but by our example. Joy and Hope are contagious, and when they grow in the midst of heartaches and trials the world will know for certain that our love for Jesus has given us pearls of great price. They will know that only a God would have the power to make men bless when they are cursed, re- joice in suffering, and give up all for the sake of the Kingdom. "As the Father has loved Me, so I have loved you. Remain in My love — so that My own joy may be in you" (Jn. 15:9, 10). The joy of Jesus will be ours, and this God-like joy Jesus needs manifested to the world through us. Love is like a fire whose sparks set aglow everything they touch, and when that love comes from God within us, it has power to prove Jesus is Lord.

Jesus Needs My Trust

The one thing that Jesus demanded of His followers was Trust. One must have a deep Faith to trust God and believe with one's whole heart that whatever happens to him is permitted by God for his good.

Jesus was always hurt when His Apostles doubted His care and Providence. He seemed to be able to endure their imperfections and weaknesses, but He was always taken aback by their lack of trust.

There are numerous occasions in Scripture when we hear Him say, "Why did you doubt? Why are you so agitated, and why are there doubts rising in your hearts?" (Lk. 24:38). It almost surprised Him that in the light of all the miracles they witnessed, they still lacked trust in His Providence.

We have all experienced the pain of a lack of trust on the part of a friend or loved one, and how uplifted we feel when a friend trusts us in a trying situation or difficult decision. The manifestation of this trust gives courage to everyone. The calm assurance of one person in a chaotic situation gives hope to all.

Jesus wants each of us to manifest a calm trust in Him during our lifetime. He needs us to manifest that trust in Him in pain, sorrow, joy, happiness, persecution, and adulation.

The world today desperately needs to see Christians maintaining trust in God's guiding hand in personal, community, and world situations. It is not a trust that is indifferent, but a trust that experiences and faces reality, and maintains an assurance that God's Love guides everything towards the good of those who love Him in return.

Everything Jesus asks of us demands our trust.

The Beatitudes are eight steps to trust, for it takes great trust to believe and live by a principle that says the poor will possess a kingdom, and the persecuted should rejoice.

It takes trust to realize that even though everything seems to be falling apart, somehow the broken pieces are in His hand, and He will put them all back together.

It takes trust to see suffering and realize that God is pruning those He loves, and Jesus Himself suffers in them.

It takes trust to pray long and hard and not receive the answer you expected.

It takes trust to realize that the things He gives us are better than the things we asked for.

It takes trust to realize that God will turn our weaknesses to our good as long as we make a sincere effort to overcome them.

It takes trust to realize that the death of a loved one happened at the best time of his life.

It takes trust to leave everyone and everything in God's Hands without worry.

And, it takes trust to believe in His Love for us when we feel He is so very far away.

Yes, all of our lives we need to trust Him, and that trust will radiate like the rays of the sun, touching everyone we meet.

The trust that Jesus demanded of His followers appears almost impossible, and this very fact proves that only God would demand an heroic trust.

He asked us not to worry about tomorrow, and the sight of that kind of trust lifts up the heart of our neighbor.

He asked us to dance for joy when we are persecuted, because when we do, we show our neighbor there is a better world beyond and in that place our treasure lies.

He asked us to do the Father's Will with complete trust in the Wisdom of His plan. The sight of this kind of trust is powerful enough to give courage to our neighbor in the most trying circumstances.

He asked us to be meek and humble of heart so we would find rest for our souls; the serenity that is the fruit of that self-control becomes the envy of the world.

To trust Him is to believe Him and love Him above all things, and when our neighbor sees that kind of total surrender, he, too, desires to leave all things and follow Him.

Trust is a quality of soul that says, in season and out of season, "All is well. God loves me."

Yes, Jesus needs our trust so that He may reward us for being at peace when everything we ask is not granted, everything we have is taken away, everyone we love leaves us, and our poor souls are steeped in their own inadequacies and frailties.

Jesus told Paul His power was at its best in weakness. It took great trust on the part of Paul to believe that God's Power in him was more evident in the midst of persecutions and infirmities than in perfect health and ministerial success. But that trust in Paul has given Christians courage and strength throughout the centuries. Jesus needed Paul to show us where real holiness and power lie — in our weakness and in His strength.

It is against our human reason to believe that power is at its best in weakness. We needed to be told that mystery by God, and we needed Paul to see that mystery exemplified. And so it is in our own lives: Jesus needs to continue telling the world about the necessity and usefulness of the trials of life, and He needs each one of us to manifest that mystery by our trust in the midst of life's trials.

There is no example more beautiful than seeing someone, in the midst of pain and sorrow, say, "I trust You, Jesus." It manifests an interior power that rises above the darkness before the dawn, and keeps its eyes on the bright Morning Star, still hidden, but ever present.

Jesus Needs My Consolation

Only once in Scripture did Jesus ask something of others, and that was comfort — companionship in a time of great need — encouragement in a time of fear — empathy in a time of darkness.

Three times He asked His Apostles to "watch and pray with Him," and three times they disappointed Him (Matt. 26:37-46). He always gave but received nothing in return.

Little seems to have changed since then. We ask and receive from Him, but what do we give Him in return? In our knowledge of His Godhead and our sinner condition, we realize that we can add nothing to His Nature or Glory. This knowledge often clouds the reality of His Goodness and His Will to be loved and comforted by us. Our intellect gets in the way of our heart. We look upon Him as One who is aloof, unaware, and unconcerned.

Nothing is further from the truth. He became man that we may look to Him for comfort and He may look to us for consolation.

He desires a "togetherness" that is warm and loving. This is far from the familiarity that loses sight of His Divinity — the kind that treats Jesus as though He were mere man and never God. Love acknowledges His Divinity, and never ceases in its desire to adore and glorify Him, but love also realizes its limitations, acknowledges its weaknesses, and reaches up in perfect trust to give comfort to its Creator and Lord.

A Christian's humility waxes strong and is able to overcome the theological speculations that tell him he cannot comfort God. He is not interested in what he cannot do; he is more interested in what God *wants* him to do.

Every time he reads the Gospel of St. Matthew, he sees how he can quench Jesus' thirst in the thirsty, His hunger in the starving, His loneliness in the prisoners, and His pain in the sick.

Jesus expresses His needs in and through our neighbor, and never wants us to forget that our neighbor's needs are *His* needs. His love for us is so great that when we suffer He suffers. He desires us to accept that suffering in union with Him — and accept the comfort and help from our neighbor also as coming from Him. In this way, it is Jesus who suffers and Jesus who comforts.

All during His public ministry, we see Jesus seeking the understanding of His Apostles, and when He found them slow to understand, He was deeply hurt. He needed Peter to understand and comfort Him when He told him about His suffering and death. Instead, He received only an argument and disbelief.

He needed the ones He healed to acknowledge His Divinity, but most of them, like the nine lepers, went their way and either forgot Him or thought He was merely a Prophet.

He needed the people to accept His signs as coming from the Father; instead, they either asked for greater signs or thought He had a devil.

He became weak so they could comfort Him, but they went their way, thinking only of themselves and how much they could get from Him. He seeks now, as He sought then, our comfort and our understanding. He wants us to think of how much He is ignored by the world and comfort Him by loving words and powerful actions.

He needs us to be aware of His Presence in our neighbor, so the comfort and consolation we render him will be rendered to Jesus.

He needs to see us more aware of His sorrows than our own. There is little value in arguing on the whys and wherefores of God's need of us. We can be sure that when we do not correspond with His Grace and Love for us, we disappoint Him and deprive Him of Glory for all eternity.

We can see this clearly in the lives of Peter and Judas. Peter denied Him, but had confidence in His Mercy, and has given all mankind an example of God's forgiveness. The forgiveness Jesus extended to Peter will glorify God for all eternity. Peter's repentance was a comfort to the Resurrected Lord Jesus.

Judas's lack of confidence in His Master's forgiveness deprived Jesus of the comfort of seeing His Crucifixion bear such great fruit of repentance. What glory Judas could have given to God for all eternity, if only he had said, "I am sorry." Just imagine the comfort we would have received if we could have looked up to Heaven and said, "How great is the Mercy of our God; He forgives those who betray Him." But Judas refused to ask, refused to believe, and refused to comfort the broken Heart of Jesus—and so he ran away from God—and despaired.

How wonderful it would be if we could say to God, "Father, I'm so sorry for all the people who offend You. I wish to make up for their offenses by trying to be like Jesus—forgiving, merciful, compassionate, and full of love. I praise You for Your Mercy and Love for poor sinners, and I ask You to shower us all with Your Grace, so we may never offend You."

We must possess in the depths of our souls a sense of sorrow for all those who squander God's Grace and Mercy by lukewarmness and indifference. Our hearts must be broken at the thought of how unrequited God's Love is in the lives of so many people. We must console Him by loving Him more and let that burning love reach out and touch cold hearts in the hope that a tiny spark may set aflame the dying embers.

He needs our consolation to comfort Him, and our neighbor needs to see that compassion in order to realize how pitiful is a heart that does not love its Lord.

Jesus Needs My Gratitude

There is no sadder passage in the New Testament than the one that describes the ingratitude of the nine lepers (Lk. 17:12-18). We are so conscious of Christ's total generosity that we never think of Him being hurt over ingratitude. We forget that Jesus is human and divine. His human heart sought after justice, and justice demanded gratitude for the miracle of healing leprosy.

He wanted those lepers to realize His personal love for them when He healed them. He did not manifest His Power to obtain personal glory, and neither was He obligated to use that Power just because there was a need.

His heart was moved to pity for those lepers, and His compassionate Love reached out and touched them. This is what He wanted them to see and understand. His love for them, and the expression of that love through His miraculous powers, should have made them eternally grateful. Instead, they were concerned only about their new bodies. They forgot the Healer, the Lover, the Savior, the compassionate Father. Only one leper saw the love behind the healing. Only one leper saw God. Only one leper saw Salvation. How foolish it is to think that if God healed all the sick in the world, they would run to the Lord with open arms! Scripture affords ample proof that ninety percent would walk away healed but hardened, without love or faith. How quickly we can forget our misery and the One who took it away.

Every time Jesus used His Power to heal, it was for the purpose of increasing Faith — Faith in the recipient and in the crowds. When the healing did not serve this purpose, it was always a crushing blow to Him. He wanted their gratitude to blossom out into thanksgiving to Him as Man, and Love and Adoration to Him as God. The nine lepers turned their elation over the cure to themselves, and had no thought of Jesus as Lord and Savior. They could think only of the things they would do, and the places they would go. Their relief from pain was like a tranquilizer, dulling their minds and drying up their hearts of all affection and gratitude.

"Where are the nine?" Jesus asked (Lk. 17:17). He was surprised that out of the ten lepers only one returned to give thanks, and he was a foreigner. How sad that one who was not a member of the chosen people would be the one who proved grateful and full of faith!

Is it not true today? How many Christians ask and receive favors from God, but never thank Him. And how many sinners, who suddenly receive some small light, repent, and then spend their entire lives in loving thanksgiving!

Our neighbor needs to see us acknowledge God as the source of all the graces, blessings, and good things that come to us. He needs to see the light of Faith that goes beyond material circumstances, bringing about success and happiness. He needs to see the hidden hand of Providence, silently guiding every facet of our lives.

Our neighbor is often surprised when we thank God for the various happenings in our lives. He may see only his own efforts, and forget that God works in and through everything that touches his life, and puts upon it His stamp of approval. It is that assurance that makes the difference between a Christian and a pagan.

Jesus needs our manifestation of His Guiding Hand in our lives in order to give our neighbor the light he needs to see God in his life. Jesus saw His Father in every moment of His earthly existence, and He accepted that moment with gratitude. He expects us to do the same. He wants us to be so conscious of His Providence that our minds and hearts break out in songs of praise and thanksgiving in every circumstance.

This is often difficult and requires great Faith. It is often discouraging and requires much Hope. It is often lonely and requires intense Love. When a Faith-filled, Hopeful heart breaks out in loving thanksgiving, it is like the music of a great symphony, rising to Heaven, and delighting the Heart of God. It is the Christian's hymn of praise that rises above the heavens in joyful and sometimes plaintive tones, but always harmonized with the sweet notes of thanksgiving. It is a music heard by the whole world. Though its source is not known, its melody calms the troubled heart and quiets the anxious mind.

St. Paul said to the Thessalonians, "Pray constantly, and for all things give thanks to God, because this is what God expects you to do in Christ Jesus" (1 Thess. 5:18).

It is in Jesus that we are to acquire a spirit of gratitude for everything in our lives. When Paul made the above statement, it was in context with a correction. He was telling them to have respect for those who preach the Good News, give courage to the apprehensive, care for the weak, and be patient with everyone. He asked them not to take revenge, but to think the best of everyone, and, most of all, to be happy at all times.

It is strange that He would end this exhortation with a plea to pray and be grateful! Paul was telling them that the only way to persevere through life's trials is to pray with a grateful heart. It is this gratitude for every smile and every tear that gives courage to the weary and fainthearted.

The first Christians caught the spark of grateful enthusiasm from Paul and the other Apostles, and now Jesus needs us to send out those same sparks to everyone we meet. The world needs to see us grateful for everything that life offers, in order to realize the value of every moment of time. If we, as

Christians, portray the same hopeless attitude towards life as unbelievers, then to whom shall they go for an example and an image of God as Father and Lover?

Jesus portrayed the Father's Love and Mercy by His actions; He showed us the Father's image by His Incarnation; He showed us how to accept life's sufferings and joys by His example; and now that He has given us His Spirit, He commissions us to go out and manifest Him to the world.

We are called upon to be grateful to Jesus, as Jesus was grateful to the Father, that the world may know that Jesus is Lord, Savior, Brother, and Lover.

Radiant Light of Jesus

To be the radiant light of Jesus is the mission of each Christian. Like the twinkle of a single star on a dark night, the Christian must give light and hope, and raise the minds and hearts of all people to the Love and Mercy of God, as Father and Lord.

The Christian's constant effort towards becoming a perfect copy of Jesus gives his neighbor hope. It fills him with a deep realization that there is an invisible reality strong enough to overcome every temptation, rise above every indignity, bear every cross, and sustain joy no matter what happens.

Jesus needs that copy, that Christian, to help radiate His Power and Personality to the world. Paul put it beautifully when He said, "God makes us, in Christ, partners of His triumph, and through us is spreading the knowledge of Himself, like a sweet smell everywhere" (2 Cor. 2:14). "We are Christ's incense to God.... You are a letter from Christ ... drawn up by the Spirit of the living God" (2 Cor. 3:2, 3). "We are ambassadors for Christ; it is as though God were appealing through us" (2 Cor. 5:20).

"We prove we are servants of God by great fortitude in time of suffering ... and by our purity, knowledge, patience, and kindness" (2 Cor. 6:4, 6).

We are so much a part of Jesus when we live the Christian life that whatever affects us affects Him, and whatever affects Him affects us. This union makes us one with our neighbor, so that whatever he suffers we suffer, and whatever he enjoys we enjoy. Paul said, "When any man has had scruples, I have had scruples with him; when any man is made to fall, I am tortured" (2 Cor. 11:29).

Because Paul was so one with Jesus, and Jesus dwelt within each Christian, Paul could say, "Now, you together are Christ's Body, but each of you is a different part of it" (1 Cor. 12:27).

"If we live by the truth and in love, we shall grow in all ways into Christ, who is the head by whom the whole Body is fitted and joined together, every joint adding its own strength for each separate part to work according to its function. So, the Body grows until it has built itself up in love" (Eph. 4:15-16).

It must have been exhilarating for these Christians, who were considered as nothing in the eyes of the world, to realize that, before God, they were important, needed, and vital members of God's saving plan. They belonged to His family. They were His sons, and, with Jesus, part of His Body, and destined for a glorious future.

"Father," Jesus said, "may they be one in Us, as You are in Me, and I am in You.... I have given them the glory You gave to Me, that they may be one as We are one" (Jn. 17:21, 22).

Jesus glorified the Father by being His perfect image, and He desires us to glorify Him by being His perfect image. Everything Jesus did was part of our Redemption. His very breath was a prayer of humility, as He lowered Himself to our human nature, and took upon Himself our weaknesses.

And so it is with us. As baptized Christians, united to Jesus, every action we perform is transformed by the Power of His Spirit, into a healing balm for the disease of sin, a consoling light for those in darkness, a comforting hope for the discouraged, and an inspirational note of joy for the saddened. United to Jesus, living His life, and Loving as He Loved, the Christian may be hidden from the eyes of the world, but the heart of the world feels every prayer and every action he performs for love of Jesus.

We are to radiate Jesus, and the rays of that light will shine to the ends of the earth, and envelop every nation and its people, because we work together with Jesus for the salvation of all mankind.

The greatest and most far-reaching light the Christian radiates to the world is the light of prayer. A Christian is never frustrated by his inability to reach men in different parts of the world. His God is everywhere, and he is a son united to his Head, Christ. He has merely to whisper a prayer of need for a fellow human being in the furthermost part of the world, and that person receives some light, some grace, some relief.

In union with Christ, the Christian is everywhere, always seeking to alleviate the needs of his brother, so that his neighbor may one day know the love of Jesus. His soul is a Temple; his mind is Christ; his heart is love. His spirit is a power that covers the world like the sun, and reaches an individual thousands of miles away, like a laser beam, healing, and giving light. The whole world is his mission; the whole world is his work; the whole world is his dwelling place; for his prayer in God reaches its farthermost ends.

"May the Peace of Christ reign in your hearts, because it is for this that you were called together as parts of one Body" (Col. 3:15).

MOTHER M. ANGELICA
(1923-2016)

Mother Mary Angelica of the Annunciation was born Rita Antoinette Rizzo on April 20, 1923, in Canton, Ohio. After a difficult childhood, a healing of her recurring stomach ailment led the young Rita on a process of discernment that ended in the Poor Clares of Perpetual Adoration in Cleveland.

Thirteen years later, in 1956, Sister Angelica promised the Lord as she awaited spinal surgery that, if He would permit her to walk again, she would build Him a monastery in the South. In Irondale, Alabama, Mother Angelica's vision took form. Her distinctive approach to teaching the Faith led to parish talks, then pamphlets and books, then radio and television opportunities.

By 1980 the Sisters had converted a garage at the monastery into a rudimentary television studio. EWTN was born.

Mother Angelica has been a constant presence on television in the United States and around the world for more than thirty-five years. Innumerable conversions to the Catholic Faith have been attributed to her unique gift for presenting the gospel: joyful but resolute, calming but bracing.

Mother Angelica spent the last years of her life cloistered in the second monastery she founded: Our Lady of the Angels in Hanceville, Alabama, where she and her Nuns dedicated themselves to prayer and adoration of Our Lord in the Most Blessed Sacrament.